Henry Cecil was born in Middlesex in 1902
and educated at King's College, Cambridge.
He was called to the Bar in 1923 and
appointed a County Court judge in 1949.
He wrote over thirty books, mainly
fiction but some serious. The best known of
his books is *Brothers in Law* which was made
into a film, a television series and several
radio series. He wrote, or collaborated
in writing, several plays which have
appeared in London's West End, the best
known of which was *Alibi for a Judge*.
Other books by him on justice and
the law are *Brief to Counsel*, *Not Such An
Ass*, *Tipping the Scales* and *The English Judge*.

Learn
about English Law

HENRY CECIL

Illustrated by
EDWARD ARDIZZONE

SPHERE BOOKS LIMITED
30/32 Gray's Inn Road, London WC1X 8JL

First published in Great Britain under the title
Know About English Law in 1965
Revised edition published by William Luscombe
Publisher Ltd, 1974
Copyright © 1965 and 1974 by Henry Cecil
Sphere Books edition published 1976
Additional material copyright © 1976 by Henry Cecil

TRADE
MARK

Set in Linotype Pilgrim

Printed in Great Britain by
Hunt Barnard Printing Ltd, Aylesbury, Bucks.

Contents

Preface to new edition 7
1 The Need for Law 9
2 Who Makes the Laws? 13
3 Gaps in the Law 18
4 Barristers and Solicitors 21
5 The Courts and the Judges 30
6 Crime and Punishment 39
7 Witnesses 48
8 The Powers of Arrest 52
9 Debtors and Creditors 55
10 Fighting a Civil Action 57
11 Unhappy Neighbours 60
12 Foster v Partridge 77
13 Conclusion 92

Preface to new edition

Since this book was first published in 1965 under the title *Know About English Law* there have been changes in the law. For example, the death penalty for murder has been abolished, the Courts have been rearranged and to some extent renamed and at least one legal anomaly has been removed. In 1965 you could be arrested without a warrant if you stole a newspaper but not if you obtained a million pounds by false pretences. This is no longer the case. It is far better not to steal or to obtain money or goods by false pretences but, if you commit any of these offences, you can be arrested without a warrant by a police officer who reasonably suspects that an offence of this kind has been committed and that you have committed it.

For just over a hundred years from 1869 an average of five thousand people a year were sent to prison (except in the years affected by the Great Wars) for not paying an ordinary debt when they had been ordered by the Court to do so and when they could have paid it if they had not used the money for some other purpose. But this was abolished in 1971 and about time too.

One of the interesting efforts of our legislators has been to abolish part-time judges called 'recorders' and replace them with part-time judges called 'Recorders'. It is, however, true to say that the jurisdiction of Recorders is greater than that of recorders.

The number of alterations in English law made it desirable

to publish a new edition of this book. It is intended as a guide to help young people and those who are completely ignorant of the English legal system to an understanding of that system, and it is hoped that, if the text is not as palatable as the author would like it to be, the splendid illustrations by Edward Ardizzone will act as a counter-attraction.

1 The Need for Law

Mr Jones, having murdered his wife, was burying her in the garden one night, when his neighbour, hearing the noise, asked him what he was doing.

'Just burying the cat,' said Mr Jones.

'Funny sort of time to bury a cat,' said the neighbour.

'Funny sort of cat,' said Mr Jones.

Now it is obvious to everyone that, in a community such as the one in which we live, some kind of law is necessary to try to prevent people like Mr Jones from killing their wives. When the world was at a very primitive stage, there was no such law, and, if a man chose to kill his wife or if a woman succeeded in killing her husband, that was their own business and no one interfered officially.

But, for a very long time now, members of every community have made laws for themselves in self-protection. Otherwise it would have meant that the stronger man could have done what he liked with the weaker, and bad men could have joined together and terrorised the whole neighbourhood.

If it were not for the law, you could not go out in broad daylight without the fear of being kidnapped, robbed or murdered. There are far, far more good people in the world than bad, but there are enough of the bad to make law necessary in the interests of everyone.

There is no difficulty in understanding this but it is just as important to understand that law is not necessary just because there are bad people in the world. If we were all as good as we ought to be, laws would still be necessary. If we never told lies, never took anything that did not belong to us, never omitted to do anything that we ought to do and never did anything that we ought not to do, we should still require a set of rules of behaviour, in other words laws, to enable us to live in any kind of satisfactory state.

How is one good man in a motor-car to pass another good man also in a motor-car coming in the opposite direction, unless there is some rule of the road? People sometimes hover in front of one another when they are walking on the pavement before they can pass, and they may even collide. Not much harm is done then, but, if two good men in motor-cars going in opposite directions hover in front of one another, not knowing which side to pass, the result will probably be that there will be two good men less in the world.

So you can see that there must be laws, however good we may be. Unfortunately, however, we are none of us always good and some of us are bad, or at any rate have our bad moments, and so the law has to provide for all kinds of possibilities. Suppose you went to a greengrocer and bought some potatoes and found on your return home that they were mouldy or even that some of them were stones, what could you do if there were no laws on the subject? In the absence of law you could only rely upon the law of the jungle. You could go back to the shop, demand proper potatoes and hit the shopkeeper on the nose if he refused to give them to you. You might then look round the shop to try to find some decent potatoes. While you were doing this, the shopkeeper might hit you on the back of the neck with a pound weight. Altogether not a very satisfactory morning's shopping.

Or you might pay your money to go to see a film at a cinema. You might go inside, sit down and wait. When the cinema was full, there might be flashed on the screen: *You've had it, Chums.* And that might be the whole of the entertainment. If there were no law, the manager could safely remain on the premises and, as you went out, smile at you and say: 'Hope you've enjoyed the show, sir.' That is to say, he could do this safely if he were bigger than you or had a well-armed bodyguard.

Every country tries, therefore, to provide laws which will help its people to live safely and as comfortably as possible. This is not at all an easy thing to do, and no country has been successful in producing laws which are entirely satisfactory. But we are far better off with the imperfect laws which we have, than if we had none at all.

The object of this book is to give you a general idea of the laws of England. They have been built up over a period of more than a thousand years and the country has, therefore, had the opportunity of learning from the mistakes of its ancestors. Younger countries have only had a far shorter time in which to develop their legal systems. The USA has had only 200 years and its system still suffers from a defect from which England once suffered. There was a stage in English history when you could bribe a judge. Even that great man Sir Francis Bacon, who (as Viscount St Albans) was Lord Chancellor from 1620 to 1622, accepted bribes, pleaded guilty to numerous charges of bribery and was sent to the Tower of London. Fortunately bribery of English judges ceased many, many years ago. There is no known case of an English judge being bribed for over 300 years. But at present a few judges in the USA do take bribes. Of course they are disgraced and sent to prison when they are caught. But it is a very difficult crime to detect. There will no doubt come a time when the USA becomes free from this defect, but it will be some years yet.

2 Who Makes the Laws?

Mr Albert Starling was a solicitor with a comfortable practice and a comfortable wife. He was fond of them both. In
addition to practising as a solicitor, he used to lecture about
law to young people in the evenings. He did this quite
voluntarily because he liked it. Frequently, before he went
to sleep, he used to tell Mrs Starling, if she was still awake,
what he was going to say in the next lecture.

'Tomorrow,' said Mr Starling, 'I'm going to talk to them
about how English laws are made.'

'Tomorrow,' said Mrs Starling, 'I'm going to buy a new
hearth-rug.'

'I'm going to tell them,' began Mr Starling and then
stopped. 'We cannot afford it,' he added. Then he went on
quickly: 'I'm going to tell them about Statute Law and
Common Law.'

'Nevertheless,' said Mrs Starling, 'I'm going to buy a new
hearth-rug.'

'Statute Law,' continued Mr Starling, ignoring his wife's
interruption, 'consists of the laws made by Parliament.
Common Law is made by the judges. Parliament is supreme
and can make as many laws as its Members are prepared to
pass.'

'I'm torn between a Persian rug and sheepskin,' said Mrs
Starling.

'Both are out of the question,' said Mr Starling. 'The Common Law consists in the laws made by the judges. The

judges of lower rank have to follow the decisions of the
judges of higher rank and, as conditions of society change,
the laws are gradually and almost imperceptibly altered by
the judges, to fit the new conditions. From time to time,
however, the conditions have changed so greatly or they
change so quickly that the judges are not able to provide for
the new situation. In all such cases Parliament can step in
and pass an Act to put the matter right. So we have these
two bodies of law, side by side, the one consisting in laws
made by Parliament and the other in laws made by the
judges. But today far less of the Common Law remains and

our lives are much more governed by Acts of Parliament
than by the laws of the judges.'

'I shall want a cheque,' said Mrs Starling. Mr Starling
locked the drawer of his desk and went on :

'Things happen so quickly today that it is of course necessary to have a body like Parliament to deal with any emergency. Such extraordinary inventions are now being made
that it is vital that Parliament should be able to control
them. It might take the judges years to do so and even then

they might not be successful. Parliament can, if necessary, pass an Act very quickly indeed. For example, suppose someone made an invention by which he could see and hear anything that was being done anywhere within a certain distance, life would become intolerable and Parliament would have to step in and prohibit the use of such an invention. But, if people who were affected by the invention sought merely to persuade the judges that it was illegal to use it, it would take a very long time to obtain such a decision and in the end the judges might hold that it was perfectly lawful to use it. After all, they might say, the man is only sitting in his own home looking and listening to his own machine. But Parliament could make that a very serious offence and, if such a machine ever should be invented, there is no doubt that a law would be made very swiftly indeed to prevent its use. This may happen sooner than we at present think.'

'How much is in the bank?' asked Mrs Starling.

'You sometimes hear it said,' said Mr Starling, 'that everyone is presumed to know the law, but this is a misunderstanding. No one can know all the law. Some judges know quite a lot about it, not always as much as they should, but still quite a lot. But even they don't know, and could not possibly know, all about all the laws. So it would be a very stupid law indeed which provided that everyone was supposed to know the law.

'What the law does say, however, is that, if you commit a crime, it is no excuse to say that you don't know it's a crime. This is a very different thing from saying that you are presumed to know the law. Everyone who commits a serious crime must know that what he is doing is wrong. Of course, there are some petty offences which someone, particularly a foreigner, might commit in ignorance. For example, a person who could not read English, might leave his car in a restricted street without knowing that this was forbidden. It is, however, in the public interest that ignorance of the law should never be a defence. Otherwise everyone charged with a minor offence might say that he did not know he was doing wrong. No injustice need be done to anyone. If a Court is satisfied that a person really did not know that he was breaking the law, it need not inflict any penalty at all upon him.'

'I am not asking you to break the law,' said Mrs Starling, 'only to sign a cheque.'

'If I signed a cheque and there were no money in my account,' said Mr Starling, 'it *might* be breaking the law. But in any event I do not agree to your buying a hearth-rug. So the question does not arise.'

He paused. Mrs Starling closed her eyes. Mr Starling continued:

'The advantage of the Common Law is this. Except in the case of an emergency it takes a long time to pass an Act of Parliament and certainly today Parliament can become overburdened with the number of Acts it is desired to pass. The Common Law, by gradually changing as conditions change, alters the law without the necessity for any Act of Parliament.

'For example, many years ago there was no water system in any house and the Common Law provided that, if a householder brought on to his land or into his house an unusual quantity of water and it leaked into somebody else's land or house, he should be liable for the damage to his neighbour's property, even if the leak was not due to any fault of his own. But today nearly every house has water stored in it and other even more dangerous things than water, for example, gas and electricity. If any of those things escape, they may hurt the next-door neighbour. But the Common Law, recognising the changing conditions, would say that, if such an escape took place without any carelessness, the person from whose house the escape took place would not be liable to his neighbour, because it is no longer unusual to keep such dangerous things in a house.

'As I have said, however, if the Common Law gets out of date and the change is so quick that the judges are unable to modify the law in time to prevent injustices, Parliament can step in and put the matter right. Now what do you think of that, my dear?'

But Mrs Starling was asleep, dreaming of a new hearth-rug.

3   Gaps in the Law

'One of the things I forgot to mention yesterday,' said Mr Starling the next night, '– are you awake, dear?'

'Unfortunately,' said Mrs Starling.

'You'll be interested in this,' said Mr Starling. 'I forgot to mention that the judges decide what Acts of Parliament mean.'

'Doesn't Parliament make their meaning plain?' asked Mrs Starling.

'Well, it tries to,' said Mr Starling, 'but not always very successfully. It seems almost impossible to make every Act of Parliament foolproof. Some of them leave out something or say something which is not plain. And in all these cases it is up to the judges to explain what the words mean and occasionally to fill in the gap and this is where we have an advantage over other countries which have no Common Law. Because in this country, when once a matter has been decided by the highest court, all the other judges follow this decision. So that everyone can know what the law is on this particular subject. In other countries they are no better at making Acts of Parliament than we are, there are still gaps in them and parts of them are difficult to understand. The result in some countries, therefore, is that no one knows for certain what the law is, because no court has to follow the decision of another court. And one judge might decide a matter one way and another judge another way. In this country at any rate we have some certainty on the matter.

'I will give you an example of the way a gap can be left in an Act of Parliament and filled by the judges. From early in the First World War until today there has been a great shortage of houses. So in 1915 Parliament passed the first Rent Restrictions Act, and this Act has continued in some form or other up till now. One object of Parliament was to prevent tenants of small houses from being turned out by their landlords except for special reasons.'

'What sort of reasons?' asked Mrs Starling.

'Failing to pay their rent or being a nuisance.'

'I should have thought that any tenant I wanted to get rid of was a nuisance,' said Mrs Starling.

'Oh no,' said Mr Starling. 'Parliament meant things like making too much noise, coming home drunk and that sort

of thing. And another reason for turning out a tenant would be if the landlord's need for the house was greater than the tenant's.'

'What did Parliament leave out?' asked Mrs Starling.

'I'm glad you're so interested,' said Mr Starling.

'I'm not,' said Mrs Starling, 'but I know you won't let me go to sleep till you've finished telling me.'

'I'll be as quick as I can,' said Mr Starling. 'Well,' he went on, 'Parliament made all the provisions that I've told you about, but it quite forgot to say that, if a tenant wanted to be protected by the Act, the house had to be his ordinary residence. As far as the actual wording of the Act was concerned, the tenant might go and live somewhere else personally, and let a relation or friend occupy the house. And, according to the Act, the tenant would still be entitled to resist the landlord's attempt to get possession of the house. So the Courts filled in the gap and held that, although the Act said nothing about it, a tenant was only protected if the house was his normal residence.'

'Good,' said Mrs Starling. 'Can I go to sleep now?'

4 Barristers and Solicitors

'You were most helpful last night,' said Mr Starling, as he got into bed the next evening. 'I brought into my lecture quite a lot of what you had said.'

'I've bought the rug,' said Mrs Starling.

'I hope it was sheepskin and not Persian,' said Mr Starling.

'You'll see,' said Mrs Starling, 'when it comes.'

Mr Starling sighed. 'Tomorrow,' he said, 'I'm going to tell them how the law is enforced and who enforces it. A law that can't be enforced is not really a law at all.'

'That's why we have all these accidents on the road, isn't it?' said Mrs Starling. 'We never go out without seeing some driver do something stupid and none of *them* is ever prosecuted.'

'You're not quite right, my dear,' said Mr Starling, 'but there is something in what you say. The trouble is that there are nothing like enough police and, as far as I can see, there never will be. People are hardly ever prosecuted except when there is actually an accident or when a policeman happens to see some bad driving. But this is just one of the misfortunes of the age. There is a law about careless driving and it can be enforced. It is simply not possible to enforce it sufficiently often. Personally, I don't think that laws will ever prevent accidents on the road. They will only be reduced when people can be *persuaded* to drive with more sense and better manners. I shall try to bring this into my lecture.'

'It might do more good than a lot of talk about judges and lawyers,' said Mrs Starling.

'None the less,' said Mr Starling, 'it is about judges and lawyers that I must talk. They play a great part in the enforcement of the law. The lawyers prepare and argue the cases, while judges and magistrates (who are junior judges) try them. Then you have the police and government inspectors, who bring cases against people who have broken the law.'

'What about juries?' said Mrs Starling.

'Quite right,' said Mr Starling. 'Juries play a great part in our criminal law. They occasionally try "civil" cases too but not very often. I will explain what a civil case is later.[1] In serious cases of crime, a person who denies his guilt is always tried by a jury – that is to say, by twelve ordinary men and women, none of whom are lawyers. A judge presides at the trial and gives them advice about the facts and tells them what the law is (or, rather, what he thinks it is). But the jury give the verdict and, if it is Not Guilty, there is nothing the judge can do about it, even if he disagrees. There once was a judge who said to a man who had been acquitted, "You are lucky in your jury." This was very wrong of the judge and an abuse of his power.'

'Is there any particular qualification to become a juryman or jurywoman?' asked Mrs Starling.

'The qualification has recently been altered. Since 31 March 1974 you must be between the ages of eighteen and sixty-five and you must also be on a Parliamentary or Local Government register of electors.'

'But do you have to be able to read?' asked Mrs Starling.

'Most jurymen can read and write,' said Mr Starling, 'but they don't have to be able to do so, provided that they have the qualifications which I have mentioned. There are certain exemptions from serving on a jury such as being a lawyer or a doctor or a clergyman and there are a few disqualifications, such as having been convicted of certain crimes. So

[1] See Page 30.

much for juries. Today I want to tell you something about the lawyers. There are two kinds of lawyer in England, barristers and solicitors. I am a solicitor.'

'Why didn't you become a barrister?' said Mrs Starling. 'You would have had your name in the papers more often.'

'I mightn't have had it in at all,' said Mr Starling. 'It used to be more difficult to succeed at the Bar than as a solicitor. Broadly speaking, the difference between a solicitor and a barrister is that the solicitor gives legal advice and prepares legal documents in connection with matters which never come to Court, such as the making of wills and the selling of land, and he prepares cases for the barrister to conduct in Court. Solicitors may in certain circumstances appear as advocates in the Crown Court and they may, whenever they wish, appear as advocates in County Courts and Magistrates' Courts, and they often do, but they also employ

barristers to do the work there. In the High Court and Courts above the High Court only a barrister can appear. Barristers are controlled by what are called Inns of Court. I'll tell you about them in a moment. Solicitors are controlled by a body called the Law Society.'

'Must a person employ a lawyer if he has a case?' asked Mrs Starling.

'No,' said Mr Starling, 'no more than you need to have an electrician to come and mend your light, but you might blow yourself up if you didn't.

'To succeed as a barrister a man must nearly always be a good advocate because so much of his work is in Court. The training of a barrister and of a solicitor is very different. I had to spend five years in a solicitor's office and take a lot of exams as well. A barrister only has to take exams. And, of course,' he added, 'eat his dinners.'

'Eat his dinners?' said Mrs Starling. 'Did you do that too?'

'No I didn't,' said Mr Starling. 'Every student who wants to become a barrister has, in addition to passing exams, to attend every so often with other students and have dinner.'

'Where?' asked Mrs Starling.

'At an Inn of Court. There are four of these Inns and they have existed for many, many years. They are the bodies which control all barristers. They are called the Inner Temple, Middle Temple, Lincoln's Inn and Gray's Inn, and every student who is called to the Bar will normally have eaten at least thirty-six dinners in his Inn.'

'That sounds a very pleasant task,' said Mrs Starling.

'It is,' said Mr Starling, 'and for over 150 years that is all a person had to do to become a barrister. There were no compulsory examinations at all. He just had to eat his dinners. But since 1872 he has had to take exams as well. The extraordinary thing is, however, that, until 1965, he did not have to have any practical experience before addressing a Court. Now he has to have six months' experience as a pupil of a practising barrister before he may plead in Court.

'A solicitor has five years' practical experience before he becomes qualified. There is this difference though. A member of the public can come straight to me. He sees my plate up, likes my name and walks in. But at any rate, even if I had only been qualified yesterday, I should have had some years of seeing how a solicitor's practice is conducted. A member of the public cannot employ a barrister direct. Only

a solicitor can employ a barrister. When he does so, he is said to "brief" him. This means that he delivers to the barrister written instructions which are called a brief. The fact that only a solicitor can brief a barrister has the effect, in many cases, of ensuring that only a barrister who is fit to take a case is employed. Because the solicitor either knows or can find out the qualifications of a barrister before he employs him.'

'But I thought you said that young George had earned £1,000 in his first year as a barrister,' said Mrs Starling.

'That's not quite right,' said Mr Starling. 'I didn't say he earned £1,000 a year. I said he had been *paid* £1,000. How much he *earned* I hesitate to say. The trouble is that sometimes solicitors, who know a young newly qualified barrister, try to help him by sending him work. Far worse than that, however, is the fact that at the moment there is a shortage of barristers to conduct cases for criminals. The result is that, if a young man goes to what is called the Criminal Bar, he is likely to get work after six months, even though he is quite unfitted to do it. The Bar was until 1965 the only profession in England where a person might practise without knowing anything about the practical side of the job. Until 1965 a barrister need never have seen the inside of a Court or a brief before he took his first case.'

'But what about a doctor?' said Mrs Starling. 'He has to have his first cut.'

'True enough,' said Mr Starling, 'but before he has his first cut, he has seen many operations conducted and has even taken a small part in them himself. The barrister who conducts his first case might (until 1965) never have seen another case conducted in his life. It is true that a barrister had from the practical point of view to become what is known as a pupil for a year, if he wished to practise in England. But during that year he was allowed to practise himself. Perhaps one day barristers will be prohibited from appearing in Court until they have had at least one year's experience of seeing other people conduct cases, though six months is very much better than nothing. The difficulty, of course, is

that today every young person wants to earn a living as soon as he or she becomes qualified. But in my view the public should be protected from the risk of its cases being conducted by someone who hasn't sufficient experience to conduct them properly. I can give you an example. Do you remember Jack Truelove?'

'Who was a boy with you, you mean?'

'Yes. Well, he became a barrister when he was twenty-one and he told me of one of his earliest experiences. He went to a Magistrates' Court to appear for a husband whose wife was asking for a separation order on the ground of his cruelty. Young Jack had no experience of such cases whatever, but for some reason or other had been briefed by a solicitor to do the case. The solicitor should have known better than to brief such an inexperienced young man. Jack travelled to the court with the solicitor and the husband. He took with him a book which had been published in the previous year and which appeared to say that the wife could not succeed in the proceedings because she was still living with her husband. Jack, full of confidence, told the solicitor and the husband that they were bound to win the case. As a result, they all had a very pleasant journey down to the Court and were almost sorry for the wife who was so ill-advised. However, it turned out that, although the book which Jack took with him correctly stated what the law was at the time it was published, the law had been changed between the date of publication and the hearing of the case. The husband duly lost but he treated Jack quite well. When they parted after the case, he only said to him, "Next time, son, get the latest edition." All the same, in the end Jack succeeded and became a successful Q.C.'

'What exactly is a Q.C.?' asked Mrs Starling.

'I'm glad you asked that,' said Mr Starling. 'Not many people outside the legal profession really know. Usually in a book or a play or a film there is a reference to a "famous Q.C.". Nearly all Q.C.s in fiction are famous, but in fact there is a good number of them of whom no one outside the legal profession has ever heard.'

'What does Q.C. stand for?' asked Mrs Starling.

'It stands for Queen's Counsel,' said Mr Starling. 'When we have a King, it is K.C. The Sovereign, on the recommendation of the Lord Chancellor, appoints barristers to this rank. They do not in fact advise the Sovereign and normally continue to act as barristers.

'But there is this difference between them and an ordinary barrister. Although an ordinary barrister appears regularly in Court, he also does a lot of work outside Court. There are a lot of technical documents which he has to prepare. Once he becomes a Q.C. he is not allowed to prepare these documents and accordingly, most of a Q.C.'s work is in Court. He, therefore, has to be a good advocate, so that a barrister, who has made a success of his job as a junior, because he is average in Court but is very good at writing the technical documents, may fail as a Q.C.'

'What is a junior?' asked Mrs Starling. 'An apprentice or something?'

'Dear me, no,' said Mr Starling. 'Ordinary barristers are known as juniors. But that does not mean they are young.

They may be very old and at one time there were quite a number with beards. Some juniors become judges without ever taking silk.'

'Taking silk?' queried Mrs Starling. 'What does that mean?'

'A Q.C. wears a silk gown,' said Mr Starling, 'while an ordinary barrister wears a stuff gown. So when a barrister becomes a Q.C. he is said to "take silk". A Q.C. is not allowed to appear in Court without having a junior with him. Accordingly, it is more expensive to have a Q.C. in your case. But it does not necessarily mean that you will have an advantage over your opponent. A good junior may be very much better than a Q.C. It all depends who they are.'

'How is one to know which is the better?' asked Mrs Starling.

'It's like an elephant,' said Mr Starling. 'I couldn't describe the one who is better, but I know him when I see him.'

5 The Courts and the Judges

Mr and Mrs Starling kept a blackboard in their bedroom. Mrs Starling used one side for her shopping list and Mr Starling used the other side to practise what he was going to put up for his pupils the next day. Sometimes they got confused, so that on one occasion the Lord Chief Justice was found curled up in the vegetables.

One night, when he could not sleep, Mr Starling got out of bed and went to the blackboard. First of all he wiped it clean. Mrs Starling appeared to be sleeping.

'There are two kinds of law in England,' said Mr Starling aloud but quietly, rehearsing his lecture. 'Civil and criminal. So there are separate civil and criminal courts. Civil courts are the courts which deal with private disputes between people or between firms and companies. Criminal courts deal with crimes. A crime may be as serious as treason or murder, or as trivial as leaving your car in the street for five minutes.'

Mrs Starling opened her eyes. 'Don't remind me,' she said. 'It cost me £2.00.'

'Cost *you*?' said Mr Starling. 'I had to pay.'

Mrs Starling shut her eyes again.

'Here are some tables of the civil and criminal courts,' said Mr Starling and he began to write on the blackboard with a piece of chalk which squeaked horribly. 'Table I shows the civil courts in their order of importance. Table II shows the way you appeal from one civil court to another. Table III shows the criminal courts in their order of import-

Table I

ORDER OF IMPORTANCE OF CIVIL COURTS

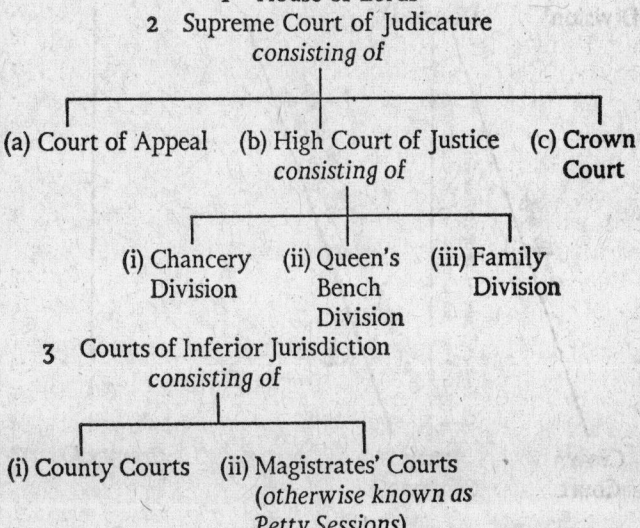

1   House of Lords

2   Supreme Court of Judicature
consisting of

(a) Court of Appeal   (b) High Court of Justice   (c) **Crown Court**
consisting of

(i) Chancery Division   (ii) Queen's Bench Division   (iii) Family Division

3   Courts of Inferior Jurisdiction
consisting of

(i) County Courts   (ii) Magistrates' Courts
(*otherwise known as Petty Sessions*)

NOTE: There is also (a) the Judicial Committee of the Privy Council composed of distinguished lawyers, nearly all judges, which advises the Sovereign on various matters. This Committee used to hear many appeals from various parts of the Commonwealth, but there are very few of these now. It also occasionally hears appeals in Church matters and by doctors who have been punished by the General Medical Council. The Committee is not strictly a Court but the effect of its decisions is the same as if it were; (b) the National Industrial Relations Court.

Table II

APPEALS IN CIVIL COURTS

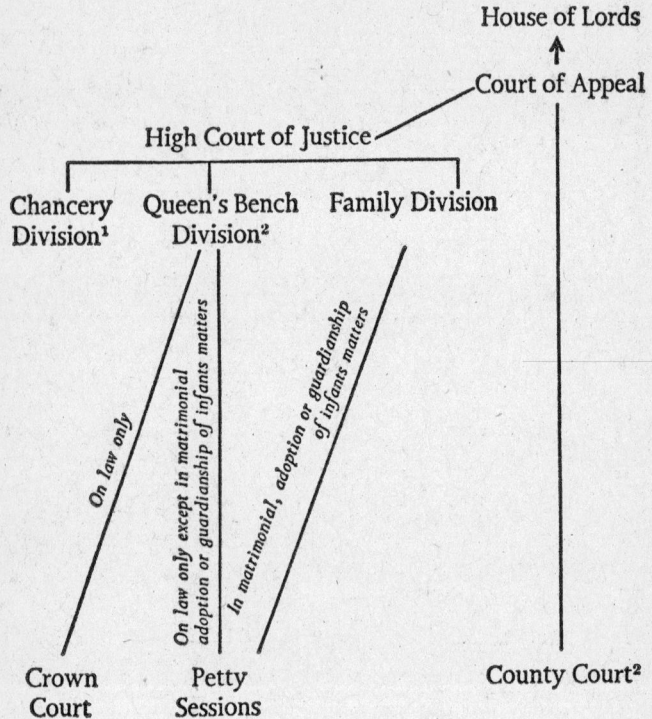

NOTE: The High Court, the County Court and Petty Sessions all deal with adoption cases.

[1] This Court deals mainly with explaining the meaning of trusts and wills, with disputed will cases, with cases about infants, e.g. adoption, with sale of land and disputes relating to limited companies.

[2] This Court deals with the ordinary cases you read about, accidents, breaches of contract, disputes between landlord and tenant, defamation cases and so forth. The County Court (with certain exceptions) deals with smaller cases of the same kind.

Table III

ORDER OF IMPORTANCE OF CRIMINAL COURTS

1   House of Lords
|
2   Court of Appeal (Criminal Division)
|
3   High Court
|
4   Crown Court
|
5   Petty Sessions

Table IV

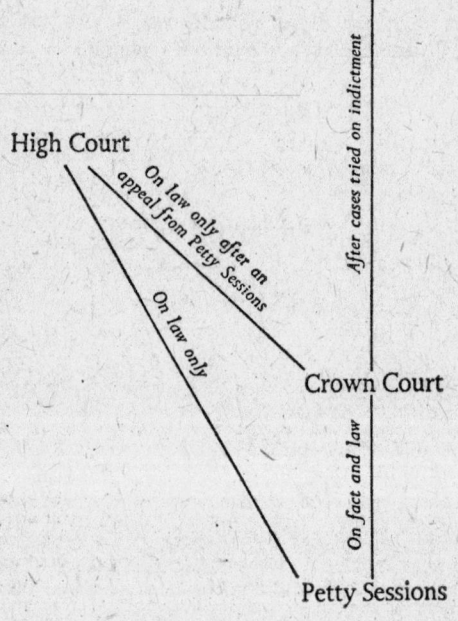

House of Lords

↑

Court of Appeal (Criminal Division)

High Court

On law only after an appeal from Petty Sessions

After cases tried on indictment

Crown Court

On law only

On fact and law

Petty Sessions

Table V

USUAL COURTS OF THE JUDGES AND COURT TITLES

Lord Chancellor	House of Lords	*My Lord*
Lord Chief Justice	Usually Queen's Bench Division or Court of Appeal (Criminal Division) but sometimes House of Lords or Court of Appeal	*My Lord*
Law Lords[1]	House of Lords	*My Lord*
Master of the Rolls[2]	Court of Appeal	*My Lord*
President of the Family Division	Family Division or occasionally Court of Appeal	*My Lord*
Lord Justice of Appeal (Lord Justice Blank)	Court of Appeal	*My Lord*
High Court Judge (Mr Justice Blank)	One of the Divisions of the High Court, the Crown Court and sometimes the Court of Appeal (Criminal Division)	*My Lord*
Circuit Judge[3] (His Honour Judge Blank)	County Court and Crown Court	Judges at the Central Criminal Court and the present Circuit Judges at Liverpool and Manchester, *My Lord.* All other Circuit Judges, *Your Honour.*
Recorders (part-time Judges)	Crown Court and County Court	*Sir*
Metropolitan Magistrates	London Magistrates' Courts	*Sir* or *Your Worship*
Stipendiary Magistrates	Certain towns outside London	*Sir* or *Your Worship*
Justices of the Peace	Petty Sessions and Crown Court	*Sir* or *Your Worship*

NOTE: Novels, films and plays frequently call judges by the wrong titles. As most members of the public do not know what the right title is, it does not make very much difference. In a television play the High Court judge who tried a criminal case was sometimes described as Judge Blank, sometimes as Lord Justice Blank and sometimes as Lord Blank. He should, of course, have been called Mr Justice Blank.

[1] Law Lords are distinguished lawyers (usually judges) who are specially made peers to hear appeals in the House of Lords.

[2] He presides over one Court of Appeal. The name is due to the fact that for many years he was responsible for the keeping of records.

[3] Circuit Judges who sit in the County Court try undefended divorce cases and short defended cases in addition to their ordinary work.

ance. Table IV shows the way you appeal from one criminal court to another. Table V shows the names of the judges, the courts they usually sit in and what they are called in Court.'

Mr Starling had to use both sides of the board for his tables and, as he finished the last one, Mrs Starling sat up and looked at it.

'You've wiped off my shopping list,' she said. 'Why can't you leave well alone?'

'You go to sleep, you old . . . ' But Mr Starling checked himself. He realised that a solicitor should not call his wife an old so-and-so. Nor, indeed, should anyone else.

'What was that you were about to say?' said Mrs Starling.

'I was about to say,' said Mr Starling hurriedly, 'that most crimes are dealt with in the Magistrates' Court.'

'It didn't sound like that,' said Mrs Starling.

'In London,' said Mr Starling, 'there are a number of Magistrates' Courts presided over by paid professional magistrates who are qualified lawyers and are called Metropolitan Magistrates. Although there are a few other qualified magistrates in the big towns who are called Stipendiary Magistrates and who are the equivalent of Metropolitan Magistrates, most Magistrates' Courts throughout the country are presided over by unpaid Justices of the Peace who are not lawyers at all. There are about 21,000 of them altogether. They have a qualified clerk to help them, and at least two justices must sit to try a case. Every criminal case starts in a Magistrates' Court but, if it is too serious for the magistrates to try, it is sent to the Crown Court to be tried by a jury. The Crown Court is presided over by a High Court or a Circuit Judge or by a Recorder, except when it hears appeals from a Magistrates' Court. In those cases not less than two and not more than four Justices of the Peace sit with the judge. The Crown Court and Magistrates' Court also deal with some civil matters such as disputes in connection with highways or rating (Crown Court) or disputes between husband and wife or landlord and tenant (Magistrates' Court).

'Justices of the Peace are appointed by the Lord Chan-

cellor on a recommendation of an advisory committee for their area. They are appointed from all classes of the population, they must be of good character and normally under sixty. They have to retire at the age of seventy and are then placed on a supplementary list when they can only discharge minor administrative duties. There are about 6,500 on this supplementary list.

'Divorces are dealt with in the High Court and County Court, but a wife whose husband has been guilty of bad conduct towards her, for example cruelty or desertion, can obtain a separation or maintenance order against him in a Magistrates' Court.

'All the most serious criminal charges are tried in the Crown Court normally before a High Court Judge. The serious but not so important cases are tried before a Circuit Judge or a Recorder in the Crown Court. The Crown Court in the City of London is known as the Central Criminal Court. It is situated in the street called Old Bailey and in consequence the court is often called 'The Old Bailey'. Many famous trials have taken place there.

'The Supreme Court of Judicature is in the Strand and civil cases are heard either there or in the High Court sitting at towns outside London or in the County Courts.'

'None of that,' said Mrs Starling, 'will help me to get your dinner for tomorrow.'

'I'll take you out to dinner,' said Mr Starling, who was sorry he had nearly called his wife something he shouldn't have.

'Darling,' said Mrs Starling.

'I've left out Coroners' Courts,' said Mr Starling. 'These are the courts where cases of accidental or unexplained death are inquired into. The proceedings are known as "an inquest". In the City of London they also hold inquests when there has been a fire, while throughout the country, when treasure is found, an inquest is held to discover who is its true owner.'

'I shouldn't mind finding some tomorrow,' said Mrs Starling. 'We could have new curtains.'

6   Crime and Punishment

We must now leave Mr and Mrs Starling and return to Mr Jones whom we met in the first chapter burying his wife in the garden. Had he been caught and convicted he would have been sentenced to imprisonment for life and the judge at the trial, if he thought fit, could have recommended how many years he should serve. But, whatever the judge's recommendation, it is a matter for the discretion of the Home Secretary how long or short a time such a prisoner remains in prison.

There is a movement for the return of the death penalty for certain offences, e.g. the killing of a prison officer or a police officer, but it is very doubtful if this movement will have any success in the near future, if at all. If, however, there were a spate of murders of police officers trying to arrest suspects, it is conceivable that Parliament might reintroduce the death penalty for such cases.

There is today a growing movement to combine punishment with reform and indeed, where possible, to substitute reform for punishment. It is admitted by most people that some criminals cannot be reformed and that for the protection of the public they must be kept under lock and key for very long periods. There are, however, many people who commit crimes who might, if properly treated, become useful citizens. It is far better that these people should, if possible, be made into useful citizens than that they should be in and out of prison all their lives, doing no good while they are in prison and doing harm while they are out.

Much more attention, too, is paid today to the mind of the person charged with crime than it used to be. And, where unfortunate people have abnormal minds or are insane or partly insane, the proper place for them is a hospital and not a prison, and today the law provides for their treatment. On the other hand, it also provides for their continued detention so long as they are likely to be dangerous to the public, if released.

Although prison has always been looked upon as a disgrace, years ago men and women and children were thrown into prison almost automatically when they were convicted of crimes, even if it was on a first conviction. Today things are very different. If anyone over twenty-one is convicted before a magistrate for the first time, the magistrate cannot send him or her to prison except for special reasons, which have to be stated. This does not apply to serious crimes which are heard at the Crown Court but only to the lesser forms of crimes which are heard before magistrates. As will be seen, even greater care is taken to prevent those under twenty-one from being sent to prison, even on a second or subsequent conviction.

For some years now, there have been what are called Juvenile Courts and anyone under the age of seventeen (who is charged by himself and not jointly with an adult) must be taken before one of these courts rather than before the ordinary Magistrates' Court. In a Juvenile Court the procedure is, as far as possible, made less alarming and everything is done to try to help the boy or girl concerned towards leading a better life in the future.

One hundred and fifty years ago children were hanged for what today would be considered petty crimes. We have gone a long way forward from then but there is still a great deal to do. Unfortunately, a large number of boys and girls do commit crimes and at the moment there are insufficient people with knowledge and experience to set them on the right road again. Officials called probation officers do a very great deal of useful work in helping children who have been brought before the courts. But there is nothing like enough of them. This will only be remedied if enough money can be found to provide proper salaries for those who are suitable to take on this work and if enough suitable people can be found to take it on. Nor are there enough places where children can, if necessary, be taken when the circumstances of their crimes or of their homes are such that they ought not to be allowed to go home immediately.

No one under the age of ten can commit a crime. Such children are presumed by the law to be too young to do so. For many years the age was eight but recently it was raised to ten.

From his tenth to his fourteenth birthday a child who has done something which would be a crime if committed by an adult is presumed by the law not to know it was wrong, unless and until it is proved that he did *in fact* know it was wrong. If this is proved, then the child can be convicted of a crime.

The law makes special provision for infants. Everyone under the age of eighteen is an infant in the eyes of the general law and is protected in certain ways by the civil law. For example, if an infant enters into a contract, in many cases it cannot be enforced against him. On the other hand, infants suffer from various disadvantages. They cannot vote at elections, they cannot marry in England without their parents' or a magistrate's consent and they have other disqualifications. Although the age of majority has been reduced from twenty-one to eighteen, no one can become a barrister or a Member of Parliament until he is twenty-one.

But in the eyes of the criminal law everyone becomes an adult at the age of seventeen, although those under twenty-one have to be much more leniently treated than those above that age. Those below the age of seventeen are divided into two groups: children (those who have not reached their fourteenth birthday) and 'young persons' (those of fourteen or more but under seventeen).

In the following paragraphs it must be remembered that 'he' is often used for convenience and includes 'she'.

Women and girls are in fact far, far more law-abiding than men and boys, but the law does not distinguish between them in fixing sentences for crimes, although the Court which sentences them has a discretion to do so. Thus a judge or magistrate who sentences a man and woman for a joint offence may punish either of them more heavily than the other. Male judges certainly tend to be more lenient with women.

Under the age of seventeen no one can be sent to prison. Instead, according to their age, children and 'young persons' may be sent to a Borstal Institution (which is described below) or to 'approved schools', detention centres or attendance centres for varying periods. Anyone of seventeen or more is treated like an adult but with two important qualifications. These are:

(1) No one between the ages of seventeen and twenty-one may be sent to prison unless the Court considers that there is no other way of dealing with the offender.

(2) Anyone of fifteen or more but under twenty-one may be sent to a Borstal Institution for a period of between nine months and two years. A Borstal Institution is a sort of training school where the inmates are locked in and are subject to strict discipline. They are taught trades or crafts, so as to enable them to earn an honest living, when released.

If a person under the age of eighteen is convicted of murder he must be sentenced to be detained in such manner as the Home Secretary may direct 'until Her Majesty's pleasure be known'. The result of such an order for detention is that the person detained may be released when the Home Secretary thinks it proper.

For adults (other than the young adults referred to) punishments for crime are as follows. For treason in wartime the punishment is death. For murder, the punishment is imprisonment for life. For other crimes an adult may be imprisoned for varying terms, fined, placed on probation or conditionally discharged. Imprisonment may be for as little

as a day or for 'life' or for very many years. A 'life' sentence does not, in fact, mean for life. The person sentenced may be released whenever the Home Secretary thinks fit, and his sentence is in any event reviewed every five years.

A fine may be as little as one half-penny or it may amount to many thousands of pounds. Both in the case of imprisonment and fine the extent of the punishment naturally depends on the nature of the crime and to some extent the past character of the person who has committed it.

An order placing someone on probation means that the person concerned must report, when required, to the probation officer and act under his directions. The order may also require the offender to comply with certain conditions, for example, to live with his parents or outside London. A probation order can only be made with the consent of the accused. Should a person refuse to consent to such an order a more severe punishment may be imposed upon him.

A conditional discharge means that the offender is let off on condition that he keeps out of trouble in the future. If he is convicted of another crime he becomes liable to be sentenced for the original crime as well.

Many thousands of people convicted for the first time are not punished at all. They are given what is called an absolute discharge. Corporal punishment has been entirely abolished. People who are found to have been insane at the time they committed what in the case of a sane person would amount to a crime are sent to a mental institution.

The Home Secretary has power to advise the Sovereign to grant a free pardon to anyone convicted of crime or to order a person to be released from prison at any time before expiry of sentence.

Sentences of imprisonment are sometimes suspended and sometimes deferred. This means that if the person convicted behaves himself during the suspension or for the period during which the sentence is deferred, he will not normally be sentenced to prison. Recently provision has also been made for what are called community service orders. These orders provide that a person instead of going to prison should do useful work for the community. At the moment it is too soon to say how successful this idea is likely to be in practice, because not every area in the country is able to provide such work. But it is obviously a good idea in principle for people who have broken the law to make up for it by helping their fellow citizens.

It is also possible for a body called the Parole Board in certain circumstances to recommend to the Home Secretary that someone be released on licence before the expiry of his sentence.

7 Witnesses

Every case has to be proved unless it is admitted, that is to say, if a man is charged with stealing something, the prosecution has to prove that he has stolen it. Or if, for example, you are claiming money from someone on the ground that you sold him a book and he has not paid for it, you must prove the sale and his failure to pay the price.

To a large extent, proof in English courts is given by word of mouth in the witness-box. What people say in the witness-box is known as evidence and evidence has to be given on oath or affirmation. The difference between an oath and an affirmation is that an oath is taken by someone who believes in a God and an affirmation by someone who either does not believe in a God or whose religion makes it wrong to take an oath or in the rare cases where a man has an unusual religion and it is not reasonably possible to administer an oath to him.

The words of the oath may vary slightly but it is usually in this form or something very near to it. 'I swear by Almighty God that the evidence which I shall give shall be the truth, the whole truth and nothing but the truth.'

Before a small boy or girl can be sworn, the judge has to satisfy himself that they realise what they are doing in taking the oath. He usually asks the child a few questions on the subject. On one occasion a boy of eight was called to give evidence and the following dialogue took place between him and the judge:

The Judge: Do you know what is meant by telling the truth?

The Boy: Yes.

The Judge: What?

The Boy: Not telling lies.

The Judge: Why not tell lies?

The Boy: Because it doesn't pay.

The Judge: Why doesn't it pay?

The Boy: Because no one would ever trust you.

This boy was the only witness of an accident and he gave his evidence as well as he had answered the judge's questions.

People sometimes wonder how much effect the oath has on a witness. On one occasion a man had made a number of

statements in Court before he had been sworn. The judge was a little suspicious of the truth of these statements and ordered that the witness should be sworn. The oath was accordingly administered to him and when he had taken it, he said at once:

4

'Now I'm on oath I'll tell the truth,' and went back on practically everything he had said.

Sometimes a witness finds it very difficult to answer questions in the witness-box and it is not always easy for a judge to tell whether the witness is merely embarrassed because he is not used to being in Court, or whether he is endeavouring not to tell the truth. On one such occasion, a witness had given several unsatisfactory answers to a judge and the judge thereupon stopped questioning him about the case and asked him this :

'Now look, Mr Blank, if you'd been the judge and I'd been the witness and I'd answered your questions as you've answered mine, what would you have thought?'

And the witness replied :

'I'd have been a bit dubious.'

You will sometimes hear people refer to the place where people give evidence as the witness 'stand'. This is an American word and should never be used in English courts. From time to time, judges growl at a young advocate who has seen so many American films on television that he asks his client to 'take the stand'. He seldom does it twice in the same court.

8 The Powers of Arrest

The general principle of English law is that a man is free and, provided he behaves himself, cannot be arrested by the police or anyone else. However, if a police officer reasonably suspects that an 'arrestable' crime has been committed, he may arrest anyone whom he reasonably suspects of having committed it. An arrestable crime is murder or any crime for which the punishment is five years' imprisonment or more. A private individual may, if any arrestable crime *has actually been committed*, arrest anyone whom he reasonably suspects of having committed it. You will see that the difference between an ordinary person's powers of arrest and that of a police officer is that the police officer need only have a reasonable suspicion that a crime has been committed, whereas a private individual may only arrest someone if a crime has in fact been committed. So it is dangerous for any ordinary citizen to arrest someone else, unless it is clear that a serious crime has been committed. Usually it is better for a private citizen to give information to a police officer and let him make the arrest, if he thinks fit.

You sometimes read that a man is 'helping the police with their inquiries'. Of course, every good citizen should want to help the police. The police are there to protect us all and in the normal way, if a policeman wants your help, you ought to give it to him.

But, when you read that someone is 'helping the police with their inquiries', it usually means that the police suspect

that man and are questioning him. The police are perfectly entitled to ask questions of people, but equally (except in certain special cases dealing with the ownership of motor-cars or that kind of thing) no one is bound to answer such questions. Still less is anyone bound to go to the police station to answer questions, unless he is arrested. But frequently people are taken to the police station when they are not under arrest. Most of these people have guilty consciences and many of them do not know that they are not bound to go. If the police were prevented from doing this, it would hamper them very much in their detection of crime. On the other hand, it does not seem satisfactory that evidence should be obtained by the police by illegal methods. One day perhaps Parliament will alter the law so that people can be questioned without the law being broken.

You may possibly have heard of the 'Judges' Rules'.

These rules were made by the judges for the purpose of trying to ensure that the police should not obtain admissions from suspects unfairly. They have recently been altered. But you may think that, if the police are allowed (as in practice they are, though in law they are not) to take people to the police station to question them, it does not make very much difference if there are all sorts of rules as to how a suspect is to be questioned.

9 Debtors and Creditors

A man who owes money to another is called a debtor and the man to whom he owes it is called a creditor. The creditor may obtain an order of the court telling the debtor to pay the money. Such an order is called a 'judgment' and once it has been obtained, the debtor is known as a 'judgment debtor' and the creditor as a 'judgment creditor'.

Over a hundred years ago judgment debtors were treated very harshly. They could be thrown into prison and could

never get out unless the debt was paid. You may have read about this in the novels of Dickens.

Just over a hundred years ago the harshness of the law was altered, but until 1971 a debtor who had been ordered by a Court to pay a sum of money to his creditor could be sent to prison for a maximum of six weeks if it was proved to the judge that he could have paid the debt or one or more of the instalments which he had been ordered to pay and had failed to do so. In 1971, however, the law was altered and no one can now be sent to prison for failing to pay any ordinary private debt. This reform was overdue. For over a hundred years an average of five thousand people who had committed no crime were sent to prison each year for no worse a sin than extravagance. But today the ordinary judgment creditor can only obtain an order against a man's employers to deduct so much a week out of his wages, if the Court thinks fit.

10 Fighting a Civil Action

One of the complaints which is most frequently made about English law is that, although everyone is theoretically entitled to bring a case before the Courts, the costs involved make it too expensive for the average person to take the risk of doing so. An oft-repeated aphorism made by a cynical judge many years ago is that 'the Courts are open to everyone, like the Ritz Hotel'.

From time to time efforts have been made to remedy this state of affairs. The most important innovation so far was the introduction of Legal Aid. This is now granted almost too generously in criminal cases, but, although it has certainly been a help to many people in civil cases, only a limited number of people can qualify to receive it. To qualify, your annual disposable income* must not exceed £950, and you must not have more than £1,200 capital.* The result is that there are many people who, though not in any sense of the word wealthy, are not able to qualify for Legal Aid. Moreover, Legal Aid is not free, unless your disposable income does not exceed £300* annually and your capital does not exceed £250.* The result is that many of those who are granted Legal Aid have to pay what is for them quite a large sum towards the expenses and although, should they win the proceedings, they may receive all or

* These amounts may be increased from time to time. 'Disposable' means after deducting allowances for rent and various other matters.

part of this back, some of them do not feel that they can afford to take the risk.

The introduction of Legal Aid has been of most use in cases of serious injury in an accident on the road or in a factory. It has also been of use in disputes between land-lords and tenants or between neighbours. But there are many other matters which though of some importance to the people concerned are of less vital importance and where, owing to the expense, people are deterred from bringing their disputes to the Courts.

In 1973 a further attempt was made by the Lord Chancellor to make it possible for small claims, mainly those not exceeding £75, to be decided by the Courts at negligible cost. An excellent booklet was issued by the Lord Chancellor's Department entitled 'Small Claims in the County Court'. It is excellent because it is simply and plainly written and designed to enable people to sue and defend actions in the County Court without a lawyer.

It is the absence of lawyers which cuts out the expense. But will the average person be able to present a case properly without legal assistance? Experience will show the extent to which people will be able to take advantage of the new procedure to conduct their own cases in the Courts. The proceedings will be in private and the strict rules which apply to ordinary cases may be considerably relaxed. But, however you may try to simplify the law, it will always be to some extent a technical matter, and a correct and just decision will in some cases only be likely to be arrived at if there are lawyers on both sides and a legally qualified tribunal.

It may be possible to improve the rules, and efforts are going on the whole time for this purpose. But in the end, if the decision in difficult cases is to be a good one, the matter will have to be argued by able lawyers. And there will not be enough of them unless they are paid well. At the moment the country cannot afford to subsidise private litigation sub-stantially more than it is doing. In the result, unless and until the State is in a position to pay all the costs of the people who go to law, fear of the expense will deter most people from exercising their legal rights. This situation is unsatisfactory but it has one advantage. This is that it is in most cases far better for people to come to an amicable agreement between themselves about their disputes than to employ lawyers to fight them out in Court.

It may nevertheless interest readers to watch an imaginary case through all its stages, from the beginning of the dispute until the eventual decision by the judge. By the time most readers have finished the story, they will have decided that a friendly chat over a glass of beer or cup of tea is far better than all the lawyers and judges in the world.

11 Unhappy Neighbours

The relationship between Mr and Mrs Foster who lived at 22 Ganymede Walk and Mr and Mrs Partridge who lived at 24 began very auspiciously. The Fosters had been in their house for some years when the Partridges arrived and they were able to be of great use to the newcomers from the moment of their actual arrival. Owing to a mistake, the Partridges' furniture was late in arriving and, if the Fosters had not very kindly offered to put them up for a week, they would have had to go to an hotel. Such a kindness should have augured well for the future, but unfortunately the two families had little in common with each other. The Fosters played bridge and were interested in all forms of sport. The Partridges, on the other hand, were fond of classical music and liked no form of sport, nor did they play cards. In consequence, they found that, when they visited each other, there was practically nothing to say unless there had been some national or local disaster. Therefore, although they were at first on perfectly good terms it was impossible for them to become real friends. Eventually trouble started.

A TV serial, with rather an attractive signature tune, was the immediate cause. Although the Fosters had no ear for music they had a piano. The only member of the family who used it was a boy aged sixteen who could not play at all well but who enjoyed strumming. After a good many unsuccessful attempts he managed to produce a rendering of the signature tune, which, though unfair to the composer, was at any rate recognisable. The boy liked the tune and so did his parents, with the result that, when he was not playing it for himself, his parents asked him to play it to them. It was a hot summer and the windows of both houses were open. Unfortunately the room in which the boy played the piano was the nearest point in the Fosters' house to the room in the Partridges' house where they used to read or listen to classical music. One very hot day, when the Partridges were listening to one of their favourite Beethoven quartets, the Foster boy started playing this signature tune, as it appeared to the Partridges, louder than ever. For a moment Mr Partridge lost control. He put his head out of the window and shouted: 'For God's sake, stop it.' Half an hour later there was a knock at the Partridges' door. It was Mr Foster.

'Did you say something?' asked Mr Foster.

'When do you mean?' parried Mr Partridge.

'You know perfectly well when I mean. About half an hour ago.'

'You mean when I asked your boy to play a little more softly?'

'You did nothing of the sort.'

'Well, we were trying to listen to some music.'

'Are we not allowed to listen to music too?'

'But he always plays the same tune.'

'We happen to like it.'

'Couldn't he close the window?'

'Why don't you close yours?'

'It's a hot day.'

'That's why he had the window open.'

'What have you come to say?'

'I've come to ask you not to shout at us through the window. If you have anything to say, kindly write it to us or call round in the normal way.'

'I'll certainly agree not to shout through the window, if you'll agree not to allow your piano to be played so loudly with the window open.'

'My boy will play that piano as loud and as long as he likes and, if you don't like it, I should find somewhere else

61

to live, if I were you. Good evening.' Mr Foster left.

That was the beginning. Before a month was out the Fosters and the Partridges spent a good deal of their time devising ways to annoy each other. One of Mr Partridge's brighter ideas was to buy a record of the signature tune. Then he opened the window in the room where they kept the gramophone, put on the record and turned the volume up as high as it would go. He put the control to 'repeat' and then he and his wife went out shopping. When they came home the gramophone was still blaring away, but there was no apparent sign of reaction from the Fosters. So Mr Partridge bought a separate loud speaker and an extra length of flex. He connected up the loud speaker to the set and took it to within a yard of the boundary between himself and the Partridges, where he concealed it in some bushes. He did not use it immediately but waited till he and his wife were going away for the week-end and then he turned it on at full blast and went off happily to the Isle of Wight.

When they came back on the Monday the record could no longer be heard. The reason for this was quite simple. Someone had cut the flex to the loud speaker extension. Then Mr Partridge noted something else. Most of his garden was covered with smuts which obviously came from a bonfire which had been lighted in the Fosters' garden. Taking advantage of what from their point of view was a favourable wind, the Fosters had lit a large bonfire which they had stoked up with paper and, when they surveyed the littered ground in the Partridges' garden, they were entirely satisfied.

But their pleasure was short-lived. They were extremely fond of their garden and particularly of their rose-bed, which they tended lovingly and with success. A fortnight after the Partridges returned from the Isle of Wight the roses appeared to be in a decline and a week after that they were all dead. The Fosters called in an expert, who diagnosed that they must have all been sprayed with a deadly poison. So the Fosters went off to their solicitors but not before they had taken advantage of another favourable wind to light an even larger bonfire than before. This sent the Partridges off to *their* solicitors.

The solicitor whom the Fosters consulted was a Mr Snape. He was an experienced man who had had a good many cases in the County Court which had arisen by reason of quarrels between neighbours. He listened sympathetically to Mr and Mrs Foster's story. When they had finished he said :

'I realise what you must have been going through. It must be quite intolerable. But I can't advise you to take proceedings yet. Before he will hear a case of this sort the judge of this Court expects the parties to have made every possible effort to try to settle the matter amicably. He says that he lives on good terms with his neighbours and he doesn't see why other people can't do the same.'

'If I had a judge for a neighbour,' said Mr Foster, 'I'd be on good terms with him.'

'No doubt,' said Mr Snape. 'I'm sure you'd find Judge Martin a very pleasant neighbour. And he certainly wouldn't poison your roses. But before you bring this case to Court, there are two things that you have got to do. First of all, you must go as pleasantly as possible to the Partridges and try and make it up. If you are successful, you won't have to come to me any more, it is to be hoped that peace will reign between you in the future and the legal costs which you have incurred will be negligible. If you fail, you will at least be able to tell the judge that you tried. For this purpose, when you come home from the unsuccessful interview, make a note of everything that was said by you and by the Partridges. The next thing you must do is to make a note of the time and date of every incident from now on and, when there is something to be seen, get as independent a person as possible to come and look at it. For example, get someone from the agents through whom you bought the house to come and have a look. If after another couple of months they are still annoying you, come back to me and I will see what I can do. But I ought to warn you that these actions are expensive. If your means are too high to entitle you to

Legal Aid, it will probably cost you at least £25 to £50 even if you win the action altogether and are awarded costs against the Partridges.'

'That's not too bad,' said Mr Foster.

'Quite so,' said Mr Snape. 'But in many of these cases the judge orders each side to pay its own costs, in which case you will certainly have to pay about £100. And, if unfortunately you should lose the action altogether, then it will cost you about £200.'

'We could manage that,' said Mr Foster.

'But,' said Mr Snape, 'I ought to warn you of this further possibility. It isn't likely but it is a possibility. You might, for example, win the action. But the judge might make some mistake in law in deciding in your favour. The other side might appeal and take you to the Court of Appeal. If you lost there, it probably might cost you £400. Moreover, the Court of Appeal might order a new trial and you might have to start all over again before this judge or another one. And the same thing could happen again after that. Finally, if you won in the Court of Appeal, it is possible that, if a point of law were involved, the other side might take it to the House of Lords. So, by the time you finished, a case like this could cost you £2,000. I don't mean that that is in the least likely. It is most unlikely. I have never in fact had a case of this kind which went to the House of Lords and only two, I think, which went to the Court of Appeal. But it is my duty to warn you of these possibilities. So, if you take my advice, you will go away and do what I have told you. And I need hardly say that the happiest thing of all for you would be if you were able to restore the good relations between you and the Partridges which I gather used to exist between you.'

Meantime, the Partridges had been going to their solicitor. He was also an experienced man and he gave them very much the same advice as Mr Snape gave to the Fosters. But he concentrated more upon the evidence to enable his clients to win the case and emphasised more than once the necessity to keep diary entries of everything that happened and to obtain witnesses whenever possible.

As a result of these interviews Mr Foster took the initiative and asked if he could call on Mr and Mrs Partridge. A meeting was arranged, but unfortunately Mr Foster started off badly by reminding the Partridges of how he had befriended them when they first came to the neighbourhood. It is human nature to resent such reminders. If you are going to remind an enemy of anything, remind him of the time when *he* helped *you*.

'That's a long time ago,' said Mr Partridge.

'Some people have short memories,' said Mr Foster.

Mr Partridge brought out his pocket book. 'I forget how much you charge for board and lodging,' he said. 'But things weren't so expensive then as they are now. Would a ten pound note help, d'you think?'

'We don't keep a common lodging house,' said Mr Foster.

'Certainly not,' said Mr Partridge. 'I wouldn't dream of suggesting it. Personally I'd advertise it as having all home comforts. The beds are a bit short, though.'

'Was the porridge to your liking?'

'Since you ask me, it was too thin. And personally I like real cream with my porridge, not the top of the milk.'

'What about the eggs? They came from our own hens.'

'No doubt,' said Mr Partridge, 'that's where they originally came from, but their journey to us was via the deep freeze and the fridge. That didn't improve the flavour.'

'It was very good of you to put up with us for so long.'

'Beggars can't be choosers.'

'Beggars,' mused Mr Foster. 'That isn't quite the word I would have used. And now perhaps you'd like to know why I've called. To tell you the truth, we've been to our solicitor about you.'

'We've been to ours about you.'

'He said we'd got a good case.'

'So does mine.'

'He also said it might cost you thousands of pounds in the end.'

'It might cost someone that,' said Mr Partridge, 'but it won't be me.'

5

'The long and the short of it is that, unless you stop your little games, I'm going to sue you so hard that you'll probably have to leave the neighbourhood. It will be in all the local papers. That won't do you any good.'

'Doesn't that depend on the judge?'

'Certainly it does. And I'm told that this judge is a good one. It won't take him long to weigh you up. Or your wife.'

'That's a matter of opinion. As a matter of fact my wife's uncle was a judge in India.'

'Why don't you join him there?'

'He's dead.'

'Well, as far as I'm concerned you can join him *there*.'

'If you've nothing else to say, I suggest you go home.'

'I will. At any rate, I've done my best.'

'I wonder what your worst is like.'

Mr Foster returned home and spent the next hour and a half trying to record as accurately as possible the course of the interview.

During the next three months the situation between the two parties deteriorated. So far from trying to become reconciled, each side sought opportunities for annoying the other. The Partridges tried telephoning the Fosters in the middle of the night and then hanging up when a tired voice answered. The Fosters retaliated in the same way.

One day, while Mr and Mrs Foster were driving past a chemical factory and commenting on the evil smell it gave out, an idea occurred to Mr Foster. His wife readily agreed to it, bought the necessary items and then waited with her husband for the wind to be in the right direction. As soon as a satisfactory day arrived, she made up an evil-smelling concoction which she placed in a large fire-resisting bowl over a stove in the garden. It was a lovely day and the sun was very hot. Normally when the Partridges sat out in the garden in the hot sun, they delighted in the cool breeze which blew across them. On this occasion they had invited some friends to tea, but the friends had only just had time to say how lovely it was in the garden and what marvellous weather it was when they all became aware of a horrible smell.

'What on earth is this disgusting smell?' asked Mr Partridge. As he had mentioned it himself, his guests did not think it rude to agree with him about it. After a moment or two Mr Partridge said grimly: 'I think I know. Excuse me a moment.' He went straight to the Fosters' front door and knocked. Mr Foster answered.

'Anything I can do for you?' asked Mr Foster pleasantly.

'I'll get you for this,' said Mr Partridge.

'I don't understand.'

'This filthy smell coming from your garden.'

'Oh, the smell,' said Mr Foster innocently. 'I'm glad you've smelled it too. I can't think what it is. It's nothing to do with us, I assure you. Would you care to have a look in the garden?'

'I would very much,' said Mr Partridge. So Mr Foster took Mr Partridge into the garden from which the stove and bowl had been removed as soon as they had spotted Mr Partridge coming round.

'Horrible, isn't it?' said Mr Foster. 'I didn't know there was a chemical factory in the area.'

'There isn't,' said Mr Partridge.

'Is there anything else you'd like to see? If it goes on, I propose to make a complaint to the local council. Would you join me in it?'

When Mr Partridge got home he telephoned a local builder.

'Mr Perkins,' he said, 'I wonder if you could do something for me quite quickly. I want you to build me an elevated seat like a tennis umpire's chair but twice as high. It's to go in the garden. For bird-watching.'

Mr Perkins quoted an acceptable price and said that he would be very happy to oblige Mr Partridge. A fortnight later the contraption appeared in Mr Partridge's garden. Seated on the top he could see anything that took place in his neighbour's garden and, indeed, if they did not draw the curtains, in his neighbour's main bedroom.

A week later Mr Foster came round to see Mr Partridge.

'Good morning,' said Mr Foster when Mr Partridge opened the door. 'Mr Peeping-Tom Partridge, I presume.'

'You hear that?' said Mr Partridge to his wife who was only a few yards inside the door. 'He called me a peeping-tom. That's slander.'

'I heard it,' said Mrs Partridge.

'And you know it,' said Mr Foster. 'I read the other day that it was a criminal offence to spy into other people's bedrooms.'

'I've done nothing of the sort,' said Mr Partridge.

'You can tell that to the judge,' said Mr Foster. 'If you don't take that contraption down within a week, I'll sue you. It's an invasion of our privacy. Why should we have to draw the blinds during the day if we want to change in our bedroom?'

'I don't care whether you draw the blinds or not,' said Mr Partridge. 'This is my garden and I can do what I like in it. And I've noticed one thing –'

'I've no doubt,' said Mr Foster, 'that you've noticed one or two things. My wife undressing, for example.'

'How dare you!' said Mrs Partridge.

'D'you hear what the lady said?' said Mr Foster. 'How dare you!'

'What I've noticed,' said Mr Partridge, 'is that, ever since I've had this ladder seat built, there has been no more smell from your garden. That's the only reason I've put it up.'

'It would have been cheaper,' said Mr Foster, 'to come with me to the local council. Well, I shan't warn you again. Unless that thing is down within a week my solicitors will be instructed to take proceedings against you.'

Mr Foster went home, but Mr Partridge immediately made an appointment with his solicitor. He kept the appointment with his wife, and together they poured out all their troubles.

'I warned you about the expense,' said Mr Gordon, their solicitor, 'but if you really think he intends to sue you, I agree with you that it would be quite a good idea to get in first. If you are the plaintiff and he is the defendant you'll be able to tell the judge the story from your point of view instead of the other way round. That's quite an advantage. Indeed, if we get able counsel, that's a very great advantage with this judge. There are some judges who think that a plaintiff wouldn't bring a case unless he was in the right. There are others, on the other hand, who think a defendant wouldn't defend a case unless *he* was in the right.'

'I thought they were all impartial,' said Mr Partridge.

'Oh they are,' said Mr Gordon. 'At least, they try to be. But they are only human beings, you know, like you and me. And every one of us has got his likes and dislikes. I know for a fact that this judge can't bear bad smells. He will never compel a clean landlord to live with a dirty tenant. On one occasion he went round to smell for himself and it nearly bowled him over. He gave the tenant a month to put it right and said that, if it weren't put right in that time, he would have to get out, even though it meant a husband and wife and five little children being turned out of the house without anywhere else to go. So, if we start the case on this smell, we should be on a good wicket. It's a pity you can't bottle a smell so that you could take him a sample.'

'You talked about having counsel,' said Mr Partridge. 'Will that add to the expense a lot?'

'Yes,' said Mr Gordon. 'I'm afraid it will. There's no point in having counsel unless we get someone good. I could get you a young man, who has only just started and wants something to cut his teeth on, fairly cheaply, but that wouldn't be much good to you. I'd do the case much better myself and that isn't being conceited because he would do it extremely badly.'

'About how much do you think it would cost?'

'It depends how long the case takes. Sometimes these cases take a couple of days or even more.'

'What's the most it could cost?' asked Mr Partridge.

'As I explained to you last time, there isn't a "most". Ninety-nine cases out of a hundred in the County Court don't go to appeal, but the odd one does and that may double the costs.'

'What's the most it will cost if it doesn't go to appeal?' asked Mr Partridge.

'There again,' said Mr Gordon, 'that depends upon how long it takes. Of course, if you win your case and get your costs and Mr Foster can pay them –'

'Oh, he can pay them all right.'

'Well then, if you win your case and get your costs and the case lasts, say, two days and we have really good counsel I shouldn't think it would cost you more than about £50 or so. Certainly not more than £75.'

'That seems a lot to pay when I'm in the right,' said Mr Partridge.

'It is,' said Mr Gordon. 'But you're not qualified to get Legal Aid because your income is too much and the costs which the Court allows you are not as much as you'll have to spend if you want to get really good representation. It's very much worse in the United States of America where, even though you win your case, you get practically no costs against the other side.'

'I can't lose the case, can I?' said Mr Partridge.

'Oh yes,' said Mr Gordon, 'you can. I can't possibly guarantee which way the judge will decide. These cases between neighbours are extremely difficult, as I told you in the first instance. Probably even before the case starts the judge will try to persuade you and Mr Foster to agree to settle the matter and, if he makes you do that, you will have to pay your own costs.'

'What will that come to?' asked Mr Partridge.

'If the case is settled on the first day, it oughtn't to cost you more than £100.'

'It's certainly worth that to get some peace,' said Mr Partridge. 'Don't you agree, dear?'

Mrs Partridge did agree.

'Very well then,' said Mr Gordon. 'Now there are three choices. You can do the case yourself and ask the judge to refer the matter to arbitration. If he does refer it, it probably will not cost you anything. Because, even if Mr Foster decides to be legally represented, the judge probably will not allow him any costs, even if he wins. I can't guarantee that, but that's what usually happens. This is a comparatively new procedure so no one's quite sure what will happen.'

'But won't I have to prepare documents and that sort of thing?' asked Mr Partridge.

'Yes, you will,' said Mr Gordon, 'but there's not much difficulty about that and they'll help you in the Court office.'

'But I won't know the legal terms,' said Mr Partridge.

'That won't matter. In a case like this, for example, all you will have to say in your Particulars of Claim will be: I live next door to Mr Foster, the defendant, and he is always doing things to annoy me. Unless the Court stops him, he will go on doing so. The things he's done are as follows. Then you'll set out, with dates, just what he has done. No particular language is necessary. For example, take the case of the smell. Just say: We were having tea on the lawn in my garden with some friends on such and such a day when the defendant, Mr Foster, by some means or other which I don't know, created a horrible smell which blew over from his garden to mine. And then you'll set out the other incidents in exactly the same way. Where you aren't sure of the date, you'll simply say on a date about so and so. Or if you aren't sure of the time you'll say, about such and such a time. And then, at the end of the Particulars of Claim, you'll ask for what the lawyers call an injunction to stop the defendant from doing things like this in the future. The officials of the Court will help you over the technical side of the matter. Then the defendant will put in his defence and will probably add a counterclaim to it. And then you will have to put in a defence to his counterclaim.'

'How do I do that?'

'That's quite simple. You'll simply say that you deny or don't admit any of the allegations made against you. If something requires explanation, then you will give the explanation. In ordinary language. Then a date will be given for the hearing and you and your wife and any of your witnesses will attend. It will be done pretty informally in the judge's or possibly in the registrar's room.'

'But won't they ask me any questions?' said Mr Partridge.

'Oh yes. Mr Foster or his representative will be allowed to ask you questions and the judge or registrar will certainly ask you questions.'

'If you're not there, I shan't know how to answer them.'

'Even if I am there,' said Mr Gordon, 'I shan't be able to prompt you as to how to answer them.'

'You could tell me afterwards if I'd said anything wrong.'

'That might not be much help,' said Mr Gordon. 'What I can do is, if you leave something out, to try to bring your mind to it. If you make a mistake or get muddled I can try to help you over that.'

'So it is of use having you there.'

'Naturally I think so,' said Mr Gordon. 'On the whole I would say this. If you've got an absolutely cast-iron case, let's say you've lent a man a hundred pounds and you have his letter thanking you for the loan and another letter apologising for not repaying it, the probability is that you could do that case as well as me. But these cases between neighbours are never easy. You see, both parties are so angry with each other that their evidence is not always entirely reliable. In such cases a good advocate may be of considerable use.'

'And you're a good advocate?' asked Mr Partridge.

'Not particularly,' said Mr Gordon. 'That's why I would advise you, if you want to fight the case as hard as you reasonably can, to have able counsel to present it for you. But I was telling you the choices. The one is, as I have said, to do the case for yourself and for you to ask the judge or registrar to try it as an arbitrator. The second is that you should let me do the case for you. And the third is for you to have able counsel.'

'And you advise me to do that?'

'Yes,' said Mr Gordon, 'in this case I do. But it's the same as in everything else. The best things are always the most expensive. Looking at it from the worst point of view, the position is, as I have said, that, if you win the case and it takes a couple of days and you are awarded the costs, you could still have to pay anything up to £75. But if you lose the case and costs are awarded against you, it might cost you £200 or £300.'

'Well,' said Mr Partridge, 'I think we'll start. You advise me to get in before he does?'

'That's right,' said Mr Gordon. 'No – wait a moment. What's this slander you spoke of? There wasn't a witness to that?'

'Only my wife.'

'She'll do. What was the slander?'

'He said I put up this seat in the garden in order to watch his wife undressing.'

'Is that right, Mrs Partridge?'

'Certainly, I heard him.'

'Well, that's certainly actionable,' said Mr Gordon. 'But if you want to sue in respect of that, you can't start the proceedings here. At the moment you can only claim for libel and slander in the High Court. That may be altered shortly. But just now that's the law. On the other hand, if he brings the claim against you you can counterclaim for slander. This is a technical matter. The long and the short of it is that, if you start the proceedings in the County Court, you cannot put in your claim for slander. If he starts the proceedings, then you can.'

'What do you advise?'

'If he really did say that and Mrs Partridge heard him, the judge ought to award you some damages. It was only your wife who heard it, so they can't be very substantial, but he might award £50 or so. And that could help you with the costs. So, on the whole, I'm going to change my advice about your starting. I think we should wait until he starts and then we will put in this counterclaim for all the things about which you complain and, in addition, the slander.'

'Then you won't have our counsel getting up and telling our side of the case first?' said Mr Partridge.

'That's quite true,' said Mr Gordon. 'We've got to decide which is the more important. To be able to bring in your claim for slander or to have the first word. On the whole I think the slander's worth keeping because, as I say, you ought to get some damages.'

'I leave it to you, Mr Gordon,' said Mr Partridge. 'I'll be entirely advised by you.'

'All right,' said Mr Gordon. 'As soon as you hear from the solicitors for Mr Foster, come and let me know.'

Meantime, Mr Foster was consulting his solicitors, and was receiving very much the same advice from them as Mr Partridge received from Mr Gordon. Both parties would have been very much better advised to be reconciled to each other and not to waste any money upon the law and lawyers. But fortunately for the lawyers there are a lot of people like Mr Partridge and Mr Foster.

A few days later Mr Partridge received the following letter from Mr Foster's solicitors:

'We have been consulted by our client Mr Foster of 22 Ganymede Walk who has complained to us about the various acts of nuisance and annoyance of which you have been guilty towards him. We do not propose at the present moment to go into details of all these acts but there is one matter which requires immediate remedy. You have erected in your garden a sort of wooden tower which overlooks our client's garden and his house. You have obviously done this so that you can climb up the tower and spy into our client's premises. By the use of this tower you are able to look into our client's bedroom, which is not overlooked by any other house or structure. This makes it necessary for our clients to keep their blinds drawn when they are dressing or undressing even in the hot weather. It also enables you to look into our client's garden. This in our view would be a nuisance in any event but, in view of the bathing pool at the bottom of our client's garden, where our client's wife enjoys bathing in the nude, the nuisance is even more serious than it would otherwise have been. Unless you will undertake to take the tower down within seven days or alternatively undertake never to climb up it yourself or to allow anybody else to do so, our instructions are to take immediate proceedings for damages and an injunction against you. In those proceedings the particulars of the other acts of annoyance and nuisance will be duly particularised. We must ask you to let us hear from you or your solicitors in the course of the next seven days.'

Mr Partridge took that letter along to his solicitors, who wrote the following reply:

'Our client Mr Partridge of 24 Ganymede Walk has handed to us your letter dated the 3rd July last. The reason why our client erected the structure to which you refer was because of the deliberate nuisance of smell which your client created in his garden. The only way to ensure that your client did not do things of this sort was to show your client that at any time he could be observed if he did them. Our client has not looked into your client's bedroom and he has no wish to see your client's wife in the nude either bathing or in any other circumstances. We will accept service of any proceedings which you may care to institute and should tell you at once that a counterclaim will be made for nuisance and annoyance and also for slander. Your letter in fact corroborates the slander spoken. In the presence of our client's wife your client said to our client that he was using the structure in his garden for the purpose of spying on your wife while she was undressing. While you have suggested much the same thing we appreciate that you could only write upon your client's instructions and that your letter was written upon a privileged occasion. But the occasion upon which your client spoke this disgusting slander to our client was not privileged. In view of the fact that the slander has been followed up by your letter we must ask your client for an undertaking not to repeat the slander in future or use any words like it. In default of such an undertaking we shall counterclaim for an injunction in addition to damages.'

12 Foster *v* Partridge

As a result of these two letters, the case of Foster against
Partridge in the Brinkley County Court came into being.
Mr Foster's solicitors delivered Particulars of Claim contain-
ing all Mr Foster's complaints and Mr Partridge's solicitors
delivered Particulars of Defence and Counterclaim contain-
ing all Mr Partridge's complaints. Finally, Mr Foster's solicitors delivered his Defence to the Counterclaim. Eventually
the case came to be heard before Judge Martin. Mr Foster
and Mr Partridge were represented by able counsel who
were both experienced and expensive. Each of them was
paid £50 for one day's hearing and a further £30 for every
additional day. It was not exactly a coincidence that they
were each paid exactly the same amount. In the first instance the Clerk to Mr Bramley, who represented Mr Foster,
had asked only £40 and £25 a day, but he happened to
speak to the Clerk to Mr Chippendale, who was counsel for
Mr Partridge, and learned that he was getting £50 and £30 a
day.

'I'll have to put that right,' he said, and telephoned the
solicitor. 'The other side have got £50 and £30,' he said, 'and
I can't let Mr Bramley go into Court for less than his
opponent is getting.'

Mr Foster could have insisted on the clerk sticking to his
agreement to accept £40 and £25 a day, but it is not easy to
get able counsel to go to a County Court, so, after putting up
a slight show of resistance, he agreed to the higher fee.

Justice is a very precious commodity and in a perfect world it would be obtainable by everybody free of charge. Unfortunately this is a very imperfect world and in the High Court, where the standard of judge is higher than that in the County Court, the matter of representation is important but not as important as in the County Court. But there is no doubt that in the lower Court the abler and more experienced advocate will, on quite a number of occasions, win a case for the plaintiff which he could have won for the defendant if he had been briefed for him.

As soon as the case was called, Mr Bramley began to open it on behalf of Mr Foster. But when the judge had learned the nature of the case he intervened.

'I suppose,' he said, 'that every effort has been made by you and your learned opponent to try and bring this unhappy case to a happy conclusion by agreement rather than by my decision. I am quite prepared to decide this case according to law. That is what I am here for. And if I do, the probability is that either the plaintiff or the defendant is going to be extremely disappointed. In any event, the relationship between them is going to be even more unhappy in the future than it has been in the past. If there is anything I can do to help the parties to arrive at a settlement I shall be delighted to help. I have the deepest sympathy with neighbours who don't get on together. Life is so much happier for everyone when they are surrounded by smiles and not scowls.'

'I'm very much obliged to your Honour,' said Mr Bramley, 'but the solicitors on both sides have made every effort to persuade their clients to come to some amicable agreement and unfortunately it has turned out to be impossible.'

'Very well,' said the judge. 'Go on, Mr Bramley.'

'Your Honour,' said Mr Bramley, 'has had great experience of quarrels between neighbours but this case has one feature which I would call refreshingly unusual. I say "refreshingly" because complaints of noise and smell and abuse are very familiar to your Honour. But I doubt whether your Honour has yet had a case where one neighbour has erected what I may call "a folly" in his back garden. In the unlikely event of this case going down to history I think it might well be described, if Mr Partridge will forgive me, as "Partridge's folly". Mr Partridge has erected in his back garden a movable structure 25 feet high on the top of which there is a chair, a swivel chair. This enables Mr Partridge, or anybody else he authorises, to climb up the structure, sit on the top and swivel the chair so that he can look in any direction. Now my client Mr Foster's house is not overlooked by any other house so that it is quite unnecessary for him and his wife to draw the curtains when they are dressing or undressing in their bedroom. Moreover, they have a pool in their back garden and, like some other people, Mrs Foster enjoys bathing without a bathing dress, and, if the weather is suitable, basking in the sun in the same condition. Until the erection of this structure no one had any chance of seeing her, except of course her husband. But, once Partridge's folly had been erected, it was necessary for my client to keep the blinds drawn in his bedroom and quite impossible for Mrs Partridge to bathe in her usual manner. Indeed, it is quite impossible for her to bathe at all, for a respectable married woman does not want her neighbour looking at her while she is sun-bathing, even in a bathing dress. Mr Partridge has been asked either to take down the structure or to give an undertaking that neither he nor anyone else will ascend it. Both these requests have been refused. I know that the law of privacy is not in a very satisfactory state and that suggestions are being made for its being improved. But, whatever the law is, I submit that no man is entitled deliberately to spy into his neighbour's garden. For example, where there was a fence between two gardens and a man of reasonable height could look over the fence into his neighbour's garden, if it were proved that a man stood there for hours on end looking into his neighbour's garden, an injunction could be granted against him for nuisance and annoyance. As your Honour knows, it is in fact a criminal offence for a person in one house to use binoculars to watch women undressing in another house.'

'Isn't the reason that this last class of case comes within the criminal law that it is conduct likely to create a breach of the peace?' asked the judge.

'I think so,' said counsel. 'In my respectful submission, if one householder is guilty of conduct against his neighbour which is likely to cause a breach of the peace, that is as much a nuisance within the legal meaning of that term as is a nuisance by noise.'

'But in the case of noise and smell,' said the judge, 'something moves, although you can't see it, from one garden to the other. I'm not an expert in these matters, but when a noise is made in garden A it shakes the sound waves in garden B, and, when a smell is started in garden A and it permeates garden B, there are actual tiny invisible particles which move from the one garden to the other. But where a person merely looks from one garden to the other, there is no physical invasion of the second garden.'

'But, your Honour,' replied Mr Bramley, 'if a man is guilty of regularly abusing his neighbour from his own garden, he may do it so quietly that it cannot be alleged there is a nuisance from noise but, if the abuse can be heard, the offender could, in my submission, be ordered by your Honour to stop it.'

'That's probably right,' said the judge.

'If that's right,' said Mr Bramley, 'although eyes don't actually speak, the deliberate gazing by one neighbour on another for prolonged periods is, in my submission, just as much a nuisance as continuous abuse.'

'What reason does Mr Partridge give for refusing to remove the structure?'

'None, your Honour. He simply says he won't remove it.'

'Why won't the defendant remove it, Mr Chippendale?' asked the judge.

'Quite simply,' said the defendant's counsel, 'because, if he did, he would be unable to prevent the defendant from boiling up some horrible concoction in his garden which sends fumes across to my client's garden. When this smell first started, my client went round to complain to the defendant, but he denied any knowledge of it. He said that the smell must come from somewhere else. As soon as this structure was put up, the smell ceased, for the very simple reason that the defendant then knew that he could be observed.'

The judge sighed. 'Whatever the result of this case,' he said, 'I'm very sorry for both parties. They must hate each other beyond reason. But you are quite right in saying that this case has unusual features, Mr Bramley. Go on, please.'

Mr Bramley completed his opening and then he called Mr Foster to give evidence as his first witness.

Mr Foster took the oath and then proceeded to state all the complaints which he had against the Partridges and how they had started. When he had finished answering his own counsel's questions, Mr Chippendale rose to cross-examine on behalf of Mr Partridge.

'You don't like Mr Partridge, do you?' was the first question.

'Nor would you,' said Mr Foster, 'if you had a neighbour like him.'

'Let me come to this structure at once,' said counsel. 'Have you or your wife ever seen Mr Partridge or anyone else on top of it when you were in your bedroom?'

'We couldn't.'

'Why not?'

'Because we drew the curtains.'

'You could peep from behind a curtain to see who was there.'

'Any peeping in this case,' said Mr Foster, 'is done by Mr Partridge.'

'You mean that, do you?' asked counsel.

'Of course.'

'Then will you tell me of any occasion when you have seen Mr Partridge peeping?'

'I told you I couldn't. We draw the curtains.'

'Well, when you've been in the garden, have you seen him peeping?'

'We don't go in the garden more than is necessary now that he's put that up. We don't want to be spied upon all the time.'

'But, Mr Foster,' said counsel, 'a lot of neighbours don't have high hedges between them. Often there is only quite a small fence and each neighbour can see what happens in the other neighbour's garden.'

'We like our privacy,' said Mr Foster. 'We wouldn't come to a house where we couldn't have it.'

'Has your wife ever seen Mr Partridge or anyone else on the structure when she was bathing?'

'No, she hasn't,' said Mr Foster, 'for the very good reason that, since that thing was put up, she hasn't been able to bathe. It cost me £200 to make that pool and now we can't use it.'

'Why not if nobody is up in the chair?'

'Really!' said Mr Foster. 'How can we tell when somebody isn't going to go up there.'

'Now let's come to another aspect of this matter,' said Mr Chippendale. 'You came round to Mr Partridge to complain about the structure, didn't you?'

'I did indeed.'

'Did you not say to him in the presence of his wife that he used it for the purpose of spying on your wife when she was undressing in the bedroom?'

'I did not.'

'Did you not call him a peeping tom?'

'I may have done.'

'What do you understand by a peeping tom?'

'What do I understand? A tom who peeps, I suppose.'

'Peeps at what?'

'Courting couples usually, I suppose.'

'Would that be an unfair description of you and your wife in the bedroom?'

'That's our business,' said Mr Foster.

'When you called Mr Partridge a peeping tom that's what you meant, wasn't it? You meant that he used this structure for the purpose of peeping into your bedroom and seeing something which he had no business to spy upon, didn't you?'

'I wonder what you'd call your neighbour,' said Mr Foster, 'if he erected something like that in the garden next to your house.'

'You mustn't ask me questions,' said counsel. 'But as you do ask me, I should tell you quite plainly that I wouldn't have given my neighbour cause to erect such a thing. Did Mr Partridge come round to you one day before the erection of this structure and complain to you about the smell coming across from your garden into his?'

'Yes, he did.'

'And then did you invite him into your garden and show him that there was nothing in your garden which could be causing the smell?'

'Yes.'

'And didn't you suggest that it might be from somewhere else?'

'I may have.'

'Was it from somewhere else?'

Mr Foster paused. After a moment or two counsel repeated the question. 'Was it from somewhere else?'

'It could have been.'

'Was it?' repeated counsel.

'There was certainly nothing in the garden when Mr Partridge came round,' said Mr Foster.

'Isn't that because you and your wife had removed it?'

'Removed what?'

'Removed whatever it was that was giving out this smell?'

Again Mr Foster paused. Eventually he said: 'Well, I had been boiling up some glue, as a matter of fact.'

'What for?'

'I'm entitled to boil up glue if I want, aren't I?'

'What did you want to use the glue for?'

'It was some time ago.'

'I daresay it was, but, if you boiled glue in your garden, you must have had a reason for doing so. Unless it was just to annoy your neighbour. You're not a carpenter by any chance, are you?'

'No.'

'Are you a handyman?'

'What do you mean by that?'

'Are you good at doing things about the house?'

'I make my wife her early morning tea, if that's what you mean?'

'You know perfectly well I don't. Do you repair hinges on doors and that sort of thing?'

'No, I can't say I do.'

'What did you want the glue for?'

'My wife wanted it, as a matter of fact.'

'What did she want it for?'

'You will have to ask her.'

'Are you really telling me that you don't know what she wanted it for?'

As there was no immediate answer Mr Chippendale went on. 'Is she a handyman?'

'She looks after the house well.'

'But she's not a carpenter, or anything of that sort?'

'No.'

'Is she a good cook?' asked the judge.

'Very, your Honour,' said Mr Foster with enthusiasm, delighted to have a question which didn't embarrass him.

'I take it that she didn't want the glue for the cooking?' said Mr Chippendale. 'Was it just glue or did you put anything else in it?'

'I believe there was something else,' said Mr Foster.

'What was that for?'

'To make it stickier.'

'So your wife wanted something that was really sticky presumably. And you've no idea what it was she wanted?'

'I can't remember.'

'Do you agree that it made a horrible smell?'

'It wasn't very nice.'

'When Mr Partridge came round to complain, did you agree with him that it was a very nasty smell?'

'I believe I did.'

'Tell me, Mr Foster,' said counsel, 'you haven't wanted any more glue, I take it, since that structure was put up?'

'I don't think we have.'

Counsel continued to cross-examine Mr Foster about various other matters in dispute and eventually sat down.

Towards the end of Mr Foster's evidence Mrs Foster told the solicitor that she didn't feel very well and eventually she said she didn't feel capable of giving evidence. She had a splitting headache and felt sick. She would have to go home, and home she went.

After Mr Foster came out of the witness-box Mr Bramley asked if the judge would let him have a few minutes' consultation outside the Court. The judge consented readily and, as soon as Mr Foster was with his solicitor and Mr Bramley, counsel asked him: 'Why on earth didn't you tell your solicitor about the glue? You said that there was nothing of the sort that had happened.'

'I'd forgotten,' said Mr Foster lamely.

'Forgotten?' said the solicitor incredulously.

'Anyway,' said Mr Foster, 'I was on oath, so I had to tell the truth, didn't I? You wouldn't have wanted me to lie, would you?'

'No, I wouldn't,' said counsel, 'but I'm sure that Mr Snape wouldn't have let you bring the case if he'd known the truth about the glue. We'll have to try and settle this.' So Mr Bramley approached Mr Chippendale.

'Can we do anything about this case?' he said.

'I'll consider it when you've closed your case.'

'Suppose I closed it now?'

'Aren't you calling Mrs Foster?'

'I'm not, as a matter of fact.'

'She was in Court, wasn't she?'

'Yes, she was, but she's gone home. She says she doesn't feel well.'

'The glue upset her, I expect. Upset you too, I shouldn't be surprised. No, I'm afraid there's nothing to be done about this unless you withdraw the claim and pay all the costs.

85

Then I might withdraw my claim for damages on the counterclaim.'

'You seem to think you've won the case already,' said Mr Bramley.

'You're usually right,' said his opponent, 'and you're not far off it this time. Shall we go back into Court?'

They went back into Court and the judge came in.

'I'm much obliged, your Honour,' said Mr Bramley. 'That is the plaintiff's case.'

'Aren't I going to have the pleasure of hearing Mrs Foster?' asked the judge.

'I'm afraid not, your Honour.'

'But if my recollection is right, Mr Foster said that at least one question should be asked of his wife and I assume he was referring to the lady who was then in Court.'

'That is so, your Honour,' said Mr Bramley.

'But you're not calling her?'

'No, your Honour.'

'Perhaps she's gone to have a bathe,' said Mr Chippendale.

'You shouldn't be offensive, Mr Chippendale,' said the judge.

'Lighthearted rather than offensive, I hope, your Honour,' said Mr Chippendale.

'Your client has still quite a number of matters to deal with,' said the judge. 'You'd better call him to deal with them.'

Mr Partridge went into the witness-box, took the oath and gave his version of the story.

'Subject to any cross-examination by my learned friend, Mr Bramley, we can deal with the smell and the structure quite shortly. Why did you put up that revolving chair in your garden?'

'So as to prevent him from making the smell without our seeing him do it.'

'Have you ever used the chair to spy on him or his wife?'

'Never.'

'When he came round to complain about the structure, was your wife present?'

'Yes, she was.'

'What did Mr Foster say?'

'He said that I was a peeping tom and that I used the chair for the purpose of spying on his wife undressing. I told him that was slander.'

'Was there any truth whatever in it?' asked counsel.

'None whatever.'

Mr Partridge then dealt with the various other matters in dispute between the parties, and, when he had finished, Mr Bramley rose to cross-examine.

'Would you describe yourself as a normal man with the normal human frailties?' was the first question.

'I'm about average, I suppose.'

'So, presumably, when the smuts from the bonfire in Mr Foster's garden came across into your garden you were very angry.'

'Certainly I was.'

'And didn't you think of some way in which you could be revenged upon the Fosters for what you considered to be their outrageous behaviour?'

'To tell you the truth – ' began Mr Partridge.

The judge intervened.

'Yes, I'd like you to do that,' he said. 'For one thing, you swore to do so and for another it makes it so much easier for me.'

'Yes,' said Mr Partridge, 'I did wonder how to get our own back.'

'And did you find a way?'

Mr Partridge hesitated, just as Mr Foster had hesitated before referring to the glue. Counsel recognised the symptoms. They usually occurred before there emerged either something like the truth or alternatively a thumping lie. 'Can I help you?' he said. 'Mr Partridge, you thought the Fosters had deliberately sprayed your garden with black smuts from his bonfire. Didn't you think he deserved to have his garden sprayed with something in return?'

'Yes, I did.'

'And did you spray the flowers with a poisonous substance?'

'Only once.'

'Once was enough, was it not? It killed the flowers which you sprayed.'

'I expect so.'

'Do you realise,' asked the judge, 'that you could have been charged with the criminal offence of causing malicious damage to property?'

'I didn't think about that,' said Mr Partridge. 'But couldn't they be charged too? They deliberately sprayed my garden with burnt paper.'

'Did it cause any damage?'

'It was a confounded nuisance, your Honour.'

'Maybe. But it didn't kill any of the flowers or shrubs or anything of that sort, did it?'

'I can't say that it did.'

'Now what about these telephone calls?' asked counsel. 'Did you ring up Mr Foster in the middle of the night and then hang up as soon as he answered?'

'That's what he did to us.'

'Never mind what he did to you,' said counsel.

'But I do mind,' said Mr Partridge. 'We minded very much. It woke us up.'

'How did you know it was him?'

'It couldn't have been anyone else. If it had been just once, or possibly twice, obviously it might have been somebody else. But this happened for three weeks. Every other night.'

'For how long did you do it to him, then?' asked counsel.

'For about the same period.'

'Before you do it again,' said the judge, 'I suggest that you should ask your solicitor to consult the Post Office Acts to advise you whether or not that isn't a criminal offence too. If you two gentlemen go on behaving like this, you may find yourselves neighbours again but this time in prison.'

'Now let's come to the Pallisers,' said counsel.

'The signature tune you mean?' asked the judge.

'Yes, your Honour. Do you like the tune, Mr Partridge?' asked counsel.

'I did when I first heard it, but after I had heard it murdered by young Foster it nearly drove me mad.'

'Did you buy a record of it?' asked counsel.

'Yes, I did.'

'Was that before or after you were driven mad?'

'After.'

'That seems an odd thing to do.'

Mr Partridge didn't answer.

'Why did you buy a record of this tune which drove you mad?'

'I thought that, if Mr Foster liked it so much, I'd let him hear it played decently.'

'So that's why you put a loud speaker in bushes as near as possible to Mr Foster's garden, connected it to the set, turned it on as loud as possible and left it going for a week-end while you went away?'

'I wanted to discourage them from playing it.'

'You can hardly complain at their cutting the connection, can you, in those circumstances?'

'I can certainly complain. They must have trespassed in my garden to do so.'

'Only to abate an intolerable nuisance.'

'They started it.'

When Mr Partridge's evidence had been concluded, Mrs Partridge gave evidence and then each counsel addressed the judge. Finally he gave judgment.

'This is a typical case,' he said, 'of a quarrel between neighbours. But it has one refreshing feature in it. Each of the parties has come as near to telling the truth as is reasonably to be expected of people who have so much enmity towards each other. Unfortunately this is a comparatively rare occurrence. Normally in these cases I find that there is acute conflict of evidence. But here there is substantial agreement by both Mr Foster and Mr Partridge as to the incidents which took place between them. I don't think there is anything really to choose between the parties. Each of them has been guilty of actionable nuisance against the other and I shall grant an injunction against each of them to prevent them from carrying on rather in the manner of juvenile delinquents. And let me make it plain to them both that, if either of them come before me for breach of this injunction and I find the allegations proved, he will almost certainly go to prison and for quite a substantial time. Let me assure both Mr Partridge and Mr Foster that for people who have never been in prison before they will find the serving of a sentence far worse than either of them could imagine. Loss of liberty is one of the most frustrating experiences that the average human being can undergo. Moreover, they will find a smell in prison which will not be to their liking. I am quite sure that the food will not be up to the standard of Mrs Foster's or Mrs Partridge's cooking. Their lives during the past year have been unhappy owing to the hatred which they have allowed to come into their hearts. They will find three months in prison far worse than anything they have experienced in the last twelve months. Or, indeed, in the whole of their lives. I have heard from counsel that the solicitors on both sides have done their best to try to persuade their clients to arrive at a sensible settlement. Unfortunately they could not persuade their clients to take their excellent advice. Now I am going to put an end to this nonsense once and for all. If the parties cannot live in peace for the right reason – that is for love of their neighbours – they will have to live in peace in fear of the consequences of not doing so. Both parties claim damages and are entitled to them. I shall award Mr Partridge £25 in respect of the slander and Mr Foster £25 in respect of his poisoned flowers. For all the other nuisances put together I shall award each side £10 and in all the circumstances, unless counsel wish to address me on the subject I shall say that each side is to pay its own costs. Having said that, let me make one final appeal to the parties. I do this entirely for their benefit. Both parties have had the doubtful satisfaction of coming to Court and receiving a decision from me. They will now be compelled by law to behave themselves. But if instead of doing this from fear, they could decide once and for all to let the past as far as possible be forgotten and, if they can't become friends, at least become tolerant neighbours, they would find life so much happier. As I have not hesitated to criticise both sides, perhaps the parties might agree on one thing. That they disapprove of my judgment. I should be very happy to think that in this way I had started them both on new and happy lives. Someone has to take the initiative in these matters. Some people think that to say they are sorry is a sign of weakness. On the contrary, it is a sign of strength and dignity. I wonder which is the more dignified and strong of the parties, Mr Foster or Mr Partridge. This can be put to the test immediately, and I suggest that, whichever of them is the stronger and more dignified, goes here and now to the other and offers to shake him by the hand.'

The judge paused. 'Go on,' he said. 'Who's to be the first?' Rather sheepishly both of them got up at the same time. 'That's what I like to see,' said the judge. And as the parties walked towards each other, the judge added, 'Splendid. I'm sorry the Court can't provide you with a drink to celebrate the occasion, but I suggest that, as soon as you can, you go and have one outside.'

When the parties had shaken hands the judge asked the clerk to call the next case. This was a claim between two motorists in respect of an accident. The plaintiff's case was that the defendant ran into him from behind while he was stationary. The defendant's case was that the plaintiff backed into him when *he* was stationary.

There will always be quarrels beween neighbours but it is to be hoped that, when the Pearson Commission has delivered its Report, Parliament will decide that there should be automatic compensation for anyone injured in a road accident and that the time of the Court should no longer be taken up with deciding what were the real causes of an accident which took place in a split second and which few people can truly and accurately describe over six months after it took place.

13 Conclusion

Should you have a legal problem of your own you should consult a solicitor about it. It is possible that you will be able to do so without any charge or with only a very small charge, if you have sufficiently little property and earnings to entitle you to Legal Aid. For some years now, there has been a legal aid scheme by which everyone who has insufficient means to bring or defend a case may be helped to do so. He may or may not have to make a contribution towards the costs. But, if it is a civil case, he must be able to show that he has a reasonable chance of winning it. If a person is charged with a serious crime and has not the means to defend himself, he will usually be granted free legal aid, if he denies his guilt.

You must not think that this book is a substitute for legal aid. Its object is simply to give you a general idea of how the law works in England. It will not help Mr Jones of page 9 when he is charged with murder, nor will it help you if (like Mrs Starling) you leave your car where you shouldn't.

There are a lot of things which there has been no room to include, but here are a few more facts you may like to know.

For instance, you have often seen pictures of judges and barristers in wigs and gowns. The wigs have survived from the end of the seventeenth century when most well-to-do men wore wigs. Later judges and barristers kept their wigs when ordinary people gave up wearing them. The long wig,

known as the 'full-bottomed' wig, is only worn on ceremonial occasions. Normally a judge wears a smaller wig known as a 'bench' wig, while a barrister wears a rather similar wig but with many more curls in it. The robes of the judges vary with the court in which they are sitting. The Court of Appeal, Chancery and Family Division Judges wear black gowns.

You may like to know how to talk to a judge out of court, that is, if you don't know him well enough to call him by his Christian name or by his nickname of Woolly or Tiny. A High Court Judge is always made a knight, so that is easy. You call him, 'Sir George'. A Circuit Judge you would call 'Judge', though people often call him 'Judge Blank'.

If you are writing to a judge, you should address the envelope in the case of :

(a) *a Law Lord:* 'The Right Honourable Lord Blank'
(b) *a Lord Justice of Appeal:* 'The Right Honourable Sir George Blank'
(c) *a High Court Judge:* 'The Honourable Sir George Blank'
(d) *a Circuit Judge:* 'His Honour Judge George Blank'.

You will see sometimes a High Court Judge referred to as a 'puisne' judge. This is pronounced 'puny' and means a judge of a superior court other than a Chief Justice. Very few people outside the law know this.

If you are thinking of becoming a lawyer yourself, try to consult a friend who is a barrister or solicitor or judge before you make up your mind about it. He may be able to help you a great deal. The legal profession is a most important one. It involves very hard work but it is full of interest. One thing about the lawyers in England you should always remember. There is a very high standard of honesty among them. They are not at all like some of the legal characters in films, where crooked lawyers put forward false evidence and so forth. The reputable English lawyer never makes up a case for his client. He simply does the best he can with what his client tells him. When judges were corrupt, no doubt barristers and solicitors were corrupt too. But that has been changed for many, many years and, however hard reputable English lawyers may fight each other, they never indulge in trickery of any kind and, if their clients want them to be dishonest, they retire from the case.

Over seven hundred and fifty years ago Magna Carta became law, as no doubt you know from your history books. King John was forced by the barons to agree to it but he arranged with the Pope to have it annulled. However, it was re-established after John's death and it is still part of the law of England today. It is not often referred to in Court now but it established the Englishman's right to freedom and in particular to freedom from unlawful arrest and freedom to obtain justice through the Courts. It did not specifically refer to freedom of speech, though that is inherent in the word freedom. The difference between freedom of speech in Communist countries and in the West is (according to a story told by *Peterborough* in *The Daily Telegraph* of 12 June 1965) that in the West you remain free after the speech.

Magna Carta, as the foundation of civil liberty, is known and respected throughout much of the Western world and forms the basis of the freedom of the citizens of other countries as well as ours.

England has lost a good deal of its international strength in the past fifty years but its moral influence is still great. This may partly be due to its standard of justice, which has never been higher.

All Sphere Books are available at your bookshop or newsagent, or can be ordered from the following address: Sphere Books, Cash Sales Department, P.O. Box 11, Falmouth, Cornwall.

Please send cheque or postal order (no currency), and allow 19p for postage and packing for the first book plus 9p per copy for each additional book ordered up to a maximum charge of 73p in U.K.

Customers in Eire and B.F.P.O. please allow 19p for postage and packing for the first book plus 9p per copy for the next 6 books, thereafter 3p per book.

Overseas customers please allow 20p for postage and packing for the first book and 10p per copy for each additional book.